Irish Horses

Céad Míle Fáilte

Text by Max Rüeger
and Hanspeter Meier

Translated by Nora Godwin

Irish Horses

Photographed by Monique and Hans D. Dossenbach

Foreword by Michael Osborne

HART-DAVIS, MACGIBBON
GRANADA PUBLISHING
London Toronto Sydney New York

Published by Granada Publishing in
Hart-Davis, MacGibbon Ltd 1977

Granada Publishing Limited
Frogmore, St Albans, Herts AL2 2NF
and
3 Upper James Street, London W1R 4BP
1221 Avenue of the Americas, New York,
NY 10020 USA
117 York Street, Sydney, NSW 2000,
Australia
100 Skyway Avenue, Toronto, Ontario,
Canada M9W 3A6
Trio City, Coventry Street,
Johannesburg 2001, South Africa

Copyright © Hallwag AG Bern 1975
This translation © Hart-Davis,
MacGibbon Ltd 1977

ISBN 0 246 10984 X

Illustrations printed in Bern, Switzerland
by Hallwag AG

Text printed in Great Britain by
Richard Clay (The Chaucer Press) Ltd
Bungay, Suffolk

Contents

Foreword

A towering flight

Sorcerer had stiffened his neck to iron, and to slow him down was beyond me; but I fought his head away to the right, and found myself coming hard and steady at a stone-faced bank with broken ground in front of it. Flurry bore away to the left, shouting something that I did not understand. That Sorcerer shortened his stride at the right moment was entirely due to his own judgement; standing well away from the jump, he rose like a stag out of the tussocky ground, and as he swung my twelve stone six into the air the obstacle revealed itself to him and me as consisting not of one bank but of two, and between the two lay a deep grassy lane, half choked with furze. I have often been asked to state the width of the bohereen, and can only reply that in my opinion it was at least eighteen feet; Flurry Knox and Dr Hickey, who did not jump it, say that it is not more than five. What Sorcerer did with it I cannot say; the sensation was of a towering flight with a kick back in it, a biggish drop, and a landing on cee-springs, still on the downhill grade. That was how one of the best horses in Ireland took one of Ireland's most ignorant riders over a very nasty place.*

* From Somerville and Ross, see Note, p. 187.

12

The subject of this book – the Irish horse – hardly needs an introduction. Throughout the world, the mention of an Irish horse produces more than enough favourable comment to justify a book entirely devoted to it. Of course, the term 'Irish horse' conveys different things to different people. For some it will call to mind spirited thoroughbreds such as Arkle or Levmoss. For others, the stouteartedness of the Irish hunter is the epitome of all that is best in the Irish horse, while it is not a horse that springs to the mind of some, but the Connemara pony, renowned for its surefootedness and agility. And each of these types, in its own way, displays traits which stamp the Irish horse as being something quite a bit out of the ordinary.

Nowadays, with the racing and breeding of thoroughbreds becoming so international, it is less easy to maintain that there is anything special about the Irish thoroughbred. But it is not generally known that one of the factors which led indirectly to the development of the thoroughbred as we know it today was the influence that the Irish horses had in English racing circles. The speed of the Irish horses, which were known as 'Hobbies', provoked a number of English breeders during the late seventeenth century and early eighteenth century to import horses of Arab blood to improve their stock. One of these horses, the Byerley Turk, was used as a charger at the Battle of the Boyne, and was for a time at stud in Ireland before moving to stud in England. He, along with the Godolphin Barb and the Darley Arabian, was the founding father of the present day thoroughbred breed.

Today of course, a horse may be bred in Ireland, raced in France and finally go to stud in the USA. But the Irish thoroughbred has still maintained a niche of its own in the world of the steeplechaser. The first recorded steeplechase took place in Ireland in 1752. O'Callaghan and Blake took as their starting and finishing points the steeples of Buttevant and Doneraile churches, hence the origin of the word 'steeple' chase. These early 'hell for leather' riders did not specify a course between the two points but merely stated that the first home was the winner.

Gradually a more uniform system of the rules developed parallel to the organization of flat racing.

Steeplechasing in Ireland and Great Britain is a well organized and popular sport and the type of thoroughbred developed for these races is by no means the 'poor relation' of the thoroughbred used for flat-racing. The Anglo-Irish chaser is a tough muscular horse with great stamina and strength of bone. He may perhaps lack the refinements of his brother the flat-racing horse, but what he lacks in speed he makes up for in heart and sheer guts. And these are traits which are the hallmark of the Irish horse, epitomized by horses such as Arkle and L'Escargot.

The Irish Draught specifies yet another development of horsebreeding in Ireland. Although a work horse, as its name implies, the Irish Draught has not the heavy squat build of the Percheron or Clydesdale, which would entail a heavy trot and awkward gallop. In contrast, the Irish Draught is a horse of smooth action with a good trot and a fair gallop. Thus it could fulfil its role of 'jack of all trades' for the ordinary Irish farmer – plough horse, cart-horse and mount for the occasional fox hunt. The Irish Draught's docility, strength and substance were later used in the production of one of Ireland's proudest exports – the Irish hunter. The hunter usually is a cross between a thoroughbred stallion and an Irish Draught mare; it is not a distinct breed, but it does possess certain distinctive qualities which have brought it world renown. The dash and speed of the thoroughbred allied to the placidity and stamina of the Irish Draught produces a quality horse of strength and courage famed not only on the hunting field but also in the horse show arenas and Three-day Events on the European Continent and the USA.

But perhaps Ireland's most personal contribution to the equine world is the Connemara pony. Medium sized, the Connemara's endurance and agility demonstrate the influence of environment on the development of the horse, and allied to the prized characteristics of placid temperament and surefootedness they are the ideal riding horse even for the nervous beginner.

What makes the Irish horse so special? All sorts of reasons are put forward, ranging from an episcopal blessing of Irish horses by our patron St Patrick, before his death, to a subversive plot by the Irish to wreak revenge on England for her domination of so many years.

But on a more down to earth level, it is clear that Ireland does possess certain advantages for horse breeding. Our climate is mild; our winters are not too long, nor our summers too hot. Limestone is a permanent part of our soils and water, thus grass is rich in bone-building substances. And above all, there is the tradition handed down from father to son, mother to daughter, of the time-hallowed skills of breeding, and rearing horses. This is, of course, where one is inclined to wax lyrical, to eulogize the marvels of the Irish horsemen and their horses. The authors may be criticized for yielding to this 'temptation' but they join distinguished company. And indeed their fault may be mitigated because perhaps unknowingly, they have stumbled upon one of the key factors that hallmarks the Irish horse when they say, that 'the contentedness of foals in Ireland comes from the fact that they can grow up among their own kind and are *always treated as horses*'. Whilst the Irishman is proud of his horses, that is exactly what they are to him – horses. The Irishman knows that just as he cannot become a horse, so horses do not become human. Out of this realization grows a deep respect for horses, and out of this respect, love. And perhaps it is this relationship between man and animal that more than anything ensures the individuality of the Irish horse.

On browsing through this book one of the striking things about the photographs is not so much the equine subjects, but their surroundings. Many of our Continental and American friends would throw up their hands in horror at the thought of leaving their horses to herd for themselves in fields that are more rock than grass, and would shudder at the idea of entrusting three horses to a young boy. But in Ireland, apart from the 'stars' of certain studfarms and racing stables, horses are not cosseted. To pamper a horse seems to an Irishman to be almost a statement of disapproval of the Divine plan. Horses are horses, and they probably know more about looking after their needs than man will ever learn.

But the impression could also be gleaned that Ireland's horses are rough, unkempt creatures, possessing few of the characteristics so famed in song and story. And in this respect, the photographers may indeed have erred to a degree, in placing perhaps a little too much emphasis on the ordinariness of the Irish horse In reality, it is not so much the horses that are ordinary, but rather their environment and the way in which they are created. In Ireland we possess some of the finest studfarms, racing stables, sales complexes in the world, and the Dublin Horse Show is perhaps one of the best pure Horse Shows in the world. Admittedly, these cater for the elite among horses, but these are an integral part of the Irish horse scene, along with the shaggy ponies and powerful Draught horses.

It has been said that horses reflect the characters of the people closest to them, and I feel that it can be said with a fair deal of truth that the Irish horse is a reflection of the character of the Irish people as a whole. As an island, we have been less ravaged by wars and revolutions than the Continent, and as a result have had time to develop at our own pace. Irishmen do not get as emotional about people, animals or events as do their European and American counterparts. An Irishman was once asked if there was a word in Ireland to correspond to the idea of the Spanish 'mañana'? 'Yes,' he replied, 'but there isn't so much urgency about it.' The basic philosophy of the Irish horse breeder is – 'there's always tomorrow' even if it means waiting twenty years to be an overnight success! Perhaps this attitude is annoying at times, but the authors of this book seem to have grasped the reasoning behind it, as they have grasped so well the influence and the importance of the horse in Ireland.

The wealth of anecdote displays the depth of research but one, in particular, springs to mind as a fitting tail-piece. The stallion, West Australian, was being exported to France, and the mare, Darling's Day, was sent to be covered by him. She arrived just as West Australian was being loaded on to the ship, but the mating took place, the product of the union being Solon, who ensured the survival of the Matchem bloodline in Ireland – a survival brought about by a matter of luck and down to earth attitude so typical of the Irish approach to horses.

MICHAEL OSBORNE
Manager of the Irish National Stud

1

Breeds
and
Types

Indomitable old rogue

In that glimpse of the rout I had recognized the streaming chestnut mane and the white legs of the venerable Trinket, the most indomitable old rogue that had ever reared up generations of foals in the way they should not go, and I knew by repute that once she was set going it would take more to stop her than the half-demolished barricade at the entrance to the wood.

As I ran I seemed to see Trinket and her disciples hurling themselves upon Mrs Knox's phaeton and Sullivan's pony, with what results no man could tell. They had, however, first to circumnavigate the promontory; my chance was by crossing it at the neck to get to the phaeton before them . . .

The trumpeting of the donkey heralded the oncoming of the stampede; I broke my way through the last of the rhododendrons and tumbled out on to the road twenty yards ahead of the phaeton.

Sullivan's pony was on its hind legs, and Sullivan was hanging on to its head. Mrs Knox was sitting erect in the phaeton with the reins in her hand.

'Get out, ma'am! Get out!' Sullivan was howling, as I scrambled to my feet.

'Don't be a fool!' replied Mrs Knox, without moving.

The stampede was by this time confronted by the barrier. There was not, however, a moment of hesitation: Trinket came rocketing out over it as if her years were four, instead of four-and-twenty; she landed with her white nose nearly in the back seat of the phaeton, got past with a swerve and a slip up, and went away for her stable with her tail over her back, followed with stag-like agility by her last foal, her last foal but one, and the donkey, with the young cattle hard on their flying heels.*

* From Somerville and Ross, see Note, p. 187.

The breeding of thoroughbreds is the most important branch of the Irish horse-breeding industry. Typical of Irish thoroughbreds is the stallion St Alphage, now at Mylerstown Stud. He is typical not only from the point of view of pedigree, performance and appearance, but also of career. He was bought as a yearling at Newmarket and raced in England until a five-year-old. After a successful career on the race course, he was sent back to Ireland to stud

The Irish Draught was originally bred as a work horse. It therefore possesses
substance and robustness, but is not a coldblood in the general sense of the word.
Cold-blooded horses are seldom as versatile as this breed. An Irish Draught can be
recognized by its strong, bony, well-proportioned build. In temperament it is usually
quiet and affable

The Irish hunter is the product of crossing an Irish Draught with a thoroughbred. The term 'hunter' is used for a wide variety of horse and does not denote one single breed, rather a so-called 'practical cross-breed'. There are heavy-, middle- and lightweight, ladies' and small hunters. Each class differs from the other according to the amount of thoroughbred blood it possesses

Show-jumpers and military horses are hunters in origin. Middle- and lightweight hunters are usually the ones trained for top-class sport. In the past, horses with special jumping potential were usually discovered by chance among the hunter classes, but now they are bred specially as jumpers. Their progeny are trained purely for sport and are seldom used for hunting

The Irish Draught is used for breeding both other Draughts and hunters. Some are still working horses on small farms

The hunter might seem to have an easier life in that it spends the summer grazing in the fields. However, it must be ready for hard work during the hunting season which begins in autumn and continues right through the winter

Horse owners in Ireland and England use their horses not only for sporting events but also enter them for shows where their appearance, movement and schooling are judged

The life of a thoroughbred in Ireland is no different from that of a thoroughbred anywhere else in the world. The best of them have a racing career and are then sent to stud to improve the strain of their own breed, and, in the long term, that of other breeds as well

The Irish Thoroughbred

The term 'Thoroughbred' refers to all horses whose pedigrees can be traced without a break to the horses entered in the first English Studbook. Thus, all thoroughbreds in the world belong to the one breed founded in England. The special characteristics of the German, French, American and Irish thoroughbred are not features of separate breeds, but of different types of the same breed. American thoroughbreds are usually compact and sturdily-built, and most suited to shorter races; the more sinewy French thoroughbreds tend to be most successful on stayer courses, whereas the Irish type is a strong and often powerful steeplechaser with its incomparable capacity for jumping.

Nowadays the genuine Irish thoroughbred is almost exclusively a steeplechaser and to a far lesser extent a hurdler. The breeding of horses for flat races is carried out on an increasingly international scale. Thus, the differences which are still evident between thoroughbreds from various countries are fast disappearing. In the future, horses will be bred for specific purposes – for example, sprinters and stayers – irrespective of the countries in which they are bred.

This trend is more noticeable in Ireland than elsewhere, because the most suitable conditions for the breeding of racehorses are offered there, thereby attracting breeders from every part of the globe. Modern modes of transport have now made it possible for a horse, after a successful career on the racecourse, to be put to stud anywhere in the world, and then for its progeny to be sent elsewhere for training. In this way, the most successful international strains are becoming increasingly intermingled.

It is difficult, therefore, to typify the modern Irish thoroughbred; it is only possible to describe the characteristics of the earlier Irish flat racer. In Ireland, horses with stamina and endurance were the most treasured. Two-year-olds were tested for short sessions only, and it was not until a horse was three years old that it was required to show its full capacity over all distances. Relatively low training costs also made it possible to test a horse's staying power and hardiness at the age of four or even five. Racecourses as long as those in Ireland are so exacting that only the most fit – physically and psychologically – can be successful. Thanks to this system, Ireland produced a large number of well-proportioned horses, which on the whole do not go in for nervous and unbalanced behaviour.

A distinctive type can still be seen today – the steeplechaser. More accurately, it should be described as the Anglo-Irish chaser, as it is bred on the same basis in both England and Ireland. This type of horse is not a fine-limbed thoroughbred with an Arabic head. It is, rather, of an athletic variety, best personified in such horses as Arkle, Red Rum and L'Escargot. This athletic type is almost perfect, for each of its features seems to have a particular function. The well-proportioned horse should have short, bony legs, a deep powerful chest and muscular hindquarters. However, temperament and character are just as vital as build for maximum performance. The even temperament and calmness of these horses, matched with a strong will and toughness, are remarkable. Note their behaviour at meetings: in the paddock before the start, the champions parade around quietly, and then, in the race, they gallop flat out, iron-like, to the finish. In the stable, too, their personality is quite evident – they seldom can be coaxed into doing anything against their will.

The fact that such a highly specialized type of thoroughbred can be trained lies in the special nature of English and Irish racing, where steeplechasing is of paramount importance. While in England approximately as many steeplechases as flat races take place, the number of steeplechases predominate in Ireland. In 1976, 882 National Hunt races were held in Ireland, and 695 flat races. However, the number of steeplechases is not the only determining factor; important too, is their nature since they are races in which the ability to jump is just as important as speed. In general, therefore, they are taken more slowly than on the Continent, particularly than in France. This difference is evident in the fact that only very few French steeplechasers have been successful in England or in Ireland, and likewise, English and Irish horses have not done well in France. Up to now, only one French steeplechaser (Lutteur III) has managed to win the Aintree Grand National. The Grand Steeplechase de Paris, the counterpart of the English Grand National, has been won on only two occasions by Anglo-Irish chasers (Troytown and Mandarin).

The reason for the predominance of steeplechasing in Ireland and England lies in the importance of the hunt. Hunting requires horses with speed and – particularly in Ireland with its many natural hurdles – with great jumping potential. As well as speed, a horse has to have staying power. A type of horse had to be bred which was suited to this hardy sport. The solution lay in crossbreeding thoroughbreds. For a thoroughbred, the necessary tempo for hunting is about a canter, whereas for most half-breds, it would mean galloping almost at full speed all the time. And the easier it is for a horse to gallop, the longer it takes for it to tire.

Although, at the outset, racehorse blood was used in the breeding of hunters, towards the beginning of the nineteenth century, steeplechasing as we know it today evolved from hunting – in a roundabout way. The horses used for this early steeplechasing came, on the one hand, from the original racing sport and, on the other, from the hunt. There must have been at one time two types or even two breeds of steeplechasers. Nowadays these two types are virtually indistinguishable. Clear differences cannot be discerned either in their jumping potential or on their appearance. The common aim in their breeding has brought about a uniform result. One can only cautiously presume that thoroughbred chasers are best in shorter races because of their speed, and half-bred chasers tend to be better over longer distances.

The following figures illustrate this point: in the approximately four and a half mile long Grand National, seven half-breds have won in the last thirty years, although they only made up a small part of the total. In the three and a quarter mile long Cheltenham Gold Cup only thoroughbreds have been winners.

The most successful, and by far the most typical representatives of these two breeds, are the horses Reynolds-

town and Arkle. The half-bred Reynoldstown is one of the two horses who managed to win the Grand National on two occasions – namely 1935 and 1936. This double success was repeated by Red Rum (also Irish bred) in 1973 and 1974. (Red Rum became the first horse to win the race a third time in 1977.) Reynoldstown's sire My Prince was a thoroughbred, and sired many successful steeplechasers. The line of his dam, Fromage, goes back to a nameless mare, whose sire Vulcan sired successful steeplechasers.

Arkle was a thoroughbred. He won the Cheltenham Gold Cup three times and the King George IV Chase once. He never ran in the Grand National, because his owner felt that the risk of injury was too high. Nevertheless he became perhaps the most famous steeplechaser of all time, winning twenty-seven races, with a grand total of £73,617 prize money. In his pedigree, he had the best blood of Irish chaser families: his sire Archive was famous as a sire of horses with great jumping ability, and his dam Bright Cherry was herself a seven-times winner over hurdles.

Because of his distinguished performance, Arkle became the most popular horse in Ireland. He perfectly embodied all the good features of Irish horses. His memory is still alive in Ireland. At every turn, and certainly in most pubs, one finds statuettes or pictures of him.

The Hunter

If a breeder's aim is to produce animals which are top of their class, he must breed them with a specific purpose in mind. This applies to all animals; cows are bred for their milk yield, sheep for quality of wool, or dogs for special tasks. Racehorses are no exception. Normally, it takes several generations of controlled breeding to produce the kind of animal desired.

It is therefore surprising that some of the world's most famous and successful horses are not the result of pure breeding, but of cross-breeding. Nearly all Irish-bred jumpers and Three-day Event horses are the descendants

The Connemara pony has evolved from the native Celtic pony which might have appeared like that pictured above, and has been influenced by warm-blooded horses such as the thoroughbred (below). However, it is now bred pure (right)

of hunters, whose sires would have been thoroughbred stallions and whose dams were Irish Draught mares. The technical term for this kind of breeding is practical cross-breeding. Experience has shown that crossing these two types has produced horses with the potential for top-performance. Thoroughbreds and Irish Draughts, both being consolidated breeds, are very compatible and this is explained by the more or less common histories of their development.

Hunting requires a robust, strong horse, that can gallop relatively effortlessly for hours on end, and furthermore can jump. A hunter also has to have a suitable temperament. Once all these qualities had been generated, different types of hunter could be bred, for example, heavier or lighter horses to suit the rider's weight or the kind of terrain involved.

There are four main showing-classes of hunter today: heavy-, middle- and lightweight hunters, and the small hunter. The latter normally has some pony blood and is intended for junior riders. Nevertheless it has to possess all the characteristics of a hunter if it is to be used to train young riders for the hunt.

The heavyweight hunter is usually the offspring of an Irish Draught mare and a thoroughbred stallion. It is distinguishable by its strength and size and is pleasant to ride, even on the most heavy-going surface. It is known for its quiet character, even temperament and reliability.

Middle- and lightweight hunters are more purely bred. Most of them are the offspring of hunter mares (themselves the result of cross-breeding) and thoroughbred stallions. They could be described as the 'nobility' among hunters.

To specify the hunter 'type', it is best to look at the criteria by which horses in each of these hunter classes are judged. These showing classes, which have been in existence in Ireland for more than a hundred years, have helped to examine the hunter type more closely, and to adjust the breeding process accordingly. Brood mares and young foals are judged by physical appearance and movement only, but most older hunters are also ridden by the judges. This serves not only to test the horse's adaptability to strange riders – a quality of prime importance on

Left: Piebald ponies are common in Ireland. Most of them are bred and owned by travelling people. This stallion, although typical of his breed, does not lead a gipsy's life, but is one of the residents of the rather high-class Ardenode stud

the hunt – but also allows a more comprehensive and objective evaluation.

There are five headings under which a horse is judged – Conformation, Action, Presence, Manners and Ride.

Conformation refers to the make and shape of a horse. It should be strong and well-balanced, standing squarely on the ground but with elegant bearing.

Under *Action*, the horse's walk and gallop are particularly scrutinized. The trot is naturally also taken into consideration but its importance is secondary.

Presence refers to how a horse generally presents itself, whether nobly and in an alert fashion, or with inertia and passivity.

Manners signifies a horse's behaviour. A hunter should be known for its pleasant temperament. A good hunter should not buck or pull, or be disturbed by the presence of other horses. Above all, it should be an easy horse to handle at the hunt.

Finally, under *Ride*, a horse's response to its rider is judged, whether its gallop can be shortened or lengthened and whether it is generally easy to control. A hunter must be able to keep up a fast gallop over a long distance and at the same time give a pleasant ride and be quiet to lead.

A further test was devised at the 1973 Dublin Horse Show. This test for the class of 'Working Hunter' requires the horse to show its aptitude for working under more exacting test conditions. As well as the usual tasks, it has to negotiate a number of fences to show its ability to jump obediently.

Because of its strictly selective breeding over the past decades, the hunter has evolved an above-average talent for jumping and eventing. Middle- and lightweight hunters rank high in this field – horses such as Gone Away, Bellevue, Mr Softee, Flanagan, Fulmer Feather Duster, Garrai Eoin, Grasshopper, Pele and East Light.

The hunt requires independent horses which can be relied upon to use their own initiative. They excel when given a free head. Some of these horses – usually the best – have a remarkably strong will and it depends on the skill of their riders to put this will to good use.

Right: The only donkey stud in the world is situated in Spanish Point on the west coast of Ireland. Patient and unpretentious, these animals pull the farmers' carts, and carry turf from the bog in large panniers. Often, in fact, a nervous horse is put to graze with a donkey, in the hope that it will take on some of the donkey's imperturbability

Irish Draught

This unique breed has become famous because, when crossed with thoroughbreds, it has produced the Irish Hunter. The Irish Draught's contribution to this cross-breed has been the inheritance of size, robustness and an even temperament.

The Irish Draught is a horse with a variety of qualities, none of which necessarily fit into the usual categories. This versatility can be explained by its history.

First and foremost it is Ireland's work and draught horse. Nevertheless, to describe it merely as a cold-blooded horse would be wrong. The Irish Draught is free of the usual characteristics of cold-blooded horses: physical and temperamental traits such as excessive weight, squat build, sluggish disposition, short walk and trot, and an awkward gallop. It is, naturally, rather strongly built and usually quite heavy, both necessary qualities of a horse meant for agricultural and draught work. However, its owner frequently uses the Irish Draught for riding or even for hunting. On the whole, Irish farmers were not wealthy enough to keep a number of horses, each with a different task. One single horse had to suffice. Hence breeders of the Irish Draught have always had as their goal a horse which would be suitable for a variety of activities.

It is not surprising that many of these horses are excellent to ride as it is likely that at some stage, thoroughbred blood was crossed into the breed. Apart from a walk and trot which cover a lot of ground, and a fast gallop, these horses frequently possess quite a talent for jumping.

It is self-evident that a horse expected to be as versatile as this will also have to meet some temperamental requirements. A stubborn, dull animal, or one that is hot-tempered and nervous, could cause problems when working. The typical Irish Draught is known for its affability and quietness.

The Irish Government's Department of Agriculture and Fisheries in its document on the horse-breeding industry in Ireland describes the Irish Draught as a powerful horse with clean limbs; it is of good quality and depth, with a height of $15\frac{1}{2}$–$16\frac{1}{2}$hh.

This could hardly be called a detailed specification, and yet it implies a great deal. An Irish Draught's appearance cannot be described feature by feature, but rather by a general overall impression. On the whole, Draughts are of well-proportioned build. Their strong bodies stand squarely on good limbs.

One reason why the official description of the Irish Draught, quoted above, is so unspecific may be because the Irish Draught has no studbook laying down the criteria of the breed. There is simply a stud register into which animals likely to produce a good strain of Draught horse are entered. Thus the title 'Irish Draught' refers to those Irish-bred horses which cannot be included in the categories of Thoroughbred, Pony, Clydesdale or Shire. The registration of Irish Draughts is now in the hands of the Irish Horse Board (Bórd na gCapall) and this organization is determined to ensure the preservation of the breed.

Because the breeding of Irish Draught horses has always been geared to more or less the same goal, the breed, although officially undefined, is unmistakable and unique, and incidentally a very likeable animal.

The Connemara Pony

The Connemara pony takes its name from its region of origin. Connemara lies north of Galway Bay along the Atlantic coast. The whole area is barren, stony and hilly, and is often swept by stormy winds. Both man and beast must struggle for existence, and this is reflected in the ponies. Hardiness and toughness are the outstanding qualities of the Connemara pony.

Unfortunately not much is known about the origins of this breed. The Celts brought ponies to Ireland around the fourth century BC, and continued to breed them in the centuries that followed. Only very few of the ponies in Connemara today, however, would be similar to these early ponies.

Some centuries later, a number of Spanish and Andalusian horses were imported into Ireland by rich Galway merchants who traded with Spain. These were crossed with the hitherto pure-bred ponies. The result was a type of small horse which was probably very similar to the present-day Connemara pony. Later, the strain was bred further, in more or less the same way.

An interesting study on the Connemara pony was written at the beginning of this century by Professor J. C. Ewart from Scotland, who was commissioned by the Department of Agriculture to look into the contemporary state of Connemara pony breeding. He held that these small horses could survive under conditions which would kill other breeds of pony. Furthermore he ascertained that they were as strong and hardy as mules, very fertile and free from hereditary diseases.

More detailed descriptions of the appearance of a Connemara pony are available from 1923 when a breeding association was set up. This society described the ponies as compact, well-proportioned horses with good bone and good movement. Their size varies from 13 to 14½hh, the average height being 13½hh.

Throughout the years, breeders have tried to develop ponies suitable for riding. Judging by the success of the Connemara pony today, their efforts have not been in vain.

A Connemara pony possesses more of the characteristics of a horse than of the pony it is generally reckoned to be. It differs from other ponies in both appearance and temperament. In build it is well-proportioned; in temperament, good-natured, docile, intelligent and often extremely determined and courageous. The usual characteristics of a pony – wide in the girth, short in the legs, heavy in the head – are not typical of the Connemara pony, nor are character-traits such as obstinacy and moodiness, which, though many pony-lovers might not admit it, are quite frequently found in ponies.

These ponies have an amazing capacity for sport – both hunting and jumping. (They can quite easily be ridden by lighter adults.) They have gained fame not only from their participation in jumping events, but also through their contribution to the breeding of other jumpers. Horses of international renown have been the result of crossing Connemara ponies with thoroughbred stallions,

horses such as Dundrum, Errigal, Smokey Joe, Little Blue Haven and Stroller.

Connemara ponies consistently show that they both possess and transmit an above-average talent for jumping. Claims that a horse will never jump of its own accord have been disproved over and over again by Connemara ponies. The innumerable stone walls which criss-cross the whole of County Galway, taking the place of hedges and fences, are frequently jumped by these small horses, often for no particular reason.

I experienced this phenomenon myself when travelling around the area with a veterinary surgeon. Whenever one of these ponies was to be brought in from the fields, it had to be approached with extreme caution, as otherwise it would simply jump over the wall and gallop away.

The vet himself was the owner of a strong and fiery pony, hardly what one would call a child's mount. As only children could compete in pony trials, he would quite happily enter his pony in events for horses. Naturally this put him at an enormous disadvantage as, for example, the distances between the fences were not measured to a pony's stride. However, this did not seem to discourage him in any way, and if the pony touched a fence, it was more likely to be with the stomach than with the legs.

2

Racing

The speed was in him

... a shot was fired at the far end of the course, everyone began to shout, and an irregularly shaped mass was detached from the crowd, and resolved itself into a group of seven horses, pounding towards us at a lumbering canter. One of the riders had a green jacket, the others were in shirt sleeves, with coloured scarves over their shoulders; all were bareheaded ...

Lyney, a square-shouldered young man, pale and long-jawed, bored determinedly on to the first flag, hit it with his right knee, wrenched Rambling Katty round the second flag, and got away for the water-jump three lengths ahead of anyone else.

'Look at that for ye – how he goes round the corner on one leg!' roared his supporter. 'He'd not stop for the Lord Leftenant!'

The remaining riders fought their way round the flags, with strange tangents and interlacing curves; all, that is to say, save the grey horse, who held on unswervingly and made straight for the river. The spectators, seated on the low bank at its edge, left their seats with singular unanimity. The majority fled, a little boy turned a somersault backwards into the water, but three or four hardier spirits tore off their coats, swung them like flails in front of the grey, and threw their caps in his face, with a wealth of objurgation that I have rarely heard equalled.

'The speed was in him and he couldn't turn,' explained one of my neighbours, at the top of his voice, as the grey, yielding to public opinion, returned to the course and resumed the race.

'That horse is no good,' said a dapper young priest, who had joined our crowd on the rock. 'Look at his great flat feet! You'd bake a cake on each of them!'

'Well, that's the case indeed, Father,' replied a grizzled old farmer, 'but he's a fine cool horse, and a great farming horse for ever. Be gance! He'd plough the rocks!'*

* From Somerville and Ross, see Note, p. 187.

48

The Irishman's great passion for gambling is often coupled with a high expertise in equestrian matters; both qualities lend a fascinating atmosphere to the whole racing scene

Around 2200 years ago, the Celts arrived in Ireland, bringing with them horses and war-chariots. There is evidence of chariot races being held, but it is only in the Brehon Laws, dating from the eighth century AD, that the first indirect references to horse-racing are made.

In the language of the Celts, a place where horse-racing was held was called a 'cuirrech'. The most famous race-course in Ireland today – the Curragh in County Kildare – still bears this name. Although there were probably many Cuirrechs, the one in Kildare even at that time must have been the most prominent.

Both the Brehon Laws and the literature from the following centuries make various references to horses, but the first mention of horse-racing is found in the account of the meeting of the King of Leinster with Richard II on the occasion of his campaign in Wicklow in 1399. This account, which is to be found in the Harleian Manuscript, gives a description of the horse which Art Mac Murchada (McMurrough) rode to this encounter. (The Curragh of Kildare would have been part of his kingdom.) The English king took particular notice of this horse, which is said to have cost its owner 400 cows. Little is known about its origin, but it is believed by some to have been imported from the Orient. It is likely to have been an ancestor of the so-called 'Hobbies', later bred by the Earl of Kildare. The Hobbies were the racehorses of medieval Ireland. Their name is probably a derivation of 'to hobble', which at that time meant to hop or dance, and which has nothing to do with the modern meaning of the word: to tie an animal's forelegs to prevent it from running away.

In 1541 Henry VIII was proclaimed King of Ireland. He is reputed to have been enthusiastic about racing. It is known that he employed a trainer, and written details exist of monies paid by him for jockeys and racing colours.

Around that time, numerous horses were imported into England from the Orient. Ireland followed this example, and thus racing developed as a sport in a similar fashion in both countries. In 1607, its growth in Ireland was arrested by an event known in Irish history as 'The Flight of the Earls'. For political reasons, many of the Irish aristocracy left the country, leaving their lands to be

Left: Have they run yet – or are they still under starter's orders? The expression on the face of this Irish racehorse displays neither disappointment nor excitement. Just let everything happen . . .

Of the thirty or so racecourses in Ireland, the Curragh and the Phoenix Park are the most famous flat racecourses. All the classic races are held in the Curragh. The most important steeplechase courses are Fairyhouse, Leopardstown and Punchestown

It is often horses starting their racing career who go over the hurdles at Naas (above) and Mallow (below). Having to ride these inexperienced horses has helped many Irish jockeys to become extremely skilful riders

58

divided among Scottish Presbyterian planters. Whereas the former landowners were enthusiastic patrons of racing, the newcomers wanted little to do with it. Interest in racing must have been high among the ordinary people because a contemporary Irish poem bemoans the fact that hunting and racing were being neglected owing to the new landowners' lack of interest. The fact that the common people could participate so actively in horse-racing is significant, and is undoubtedly one of the reasons why it managed to survive despite so many set-backs.

Towards the end of the seventeenth century, racing and subsequently the whole horse-breeding industry in Ireland suffered yet another setback. The result of the many revolts, in which the Irish took up arms against the English, was the institution of the Penal Laws, which ensured that Catholics became second-class citizens of the country. No Catholic could own a horse valued at more than five pounds. However, the enthusiasm of the Irish for horse racing managed to overcome even these political and confessional barriers. It is well known that horses of Catholic owners were often entered under a Protestant name.

Fortunately, not all aspects of the racing industry of the time were negative. Efforts continued to be made to develop it, mainly in the form of prizes offered to winners by the Duke of Leinster and King James II and later William III. It was, of course, not merely interest in racing which motivated the generosity of these monarchs, but also their practical recognition of the military and commercial importance of breeding horses capable of top performance.

It is also interesting to note that, during the Battle of the Boyne, in which he defeated James II, William III had a horse named the Byerley Turk among his chargers. The English Captain of Horse had taken this Turkish stallion as booty during the siege of Vienna by the Turks in 1683 and later rode him in William III's cavalry. The same Byerley Turk was one of the three stallions who founded the English thoroughbred stock. The Byerley Turk stood at stud in Ireland for some years after the Battle of the Boyne, before being returned to England.

It was primarily the gentry and the rich who promoted horse-racing. They were the only ones to have sufficient means to own horses of Oriental ancestry. The ordinary people had to be content with the role of onlookers. In the long run, however, it seems that this was not enough for them, as soon they began to race their own horses. These races differed from the 'official' ones in that they were purely for enjoyment, and also in that one race would involve quite a number of horses. Naturally enough the people needed their horses for working on the farm and bred them solely for this purpose – for strength rather than speed. Nevertheless the significance of these popular races should not be underestimated, as it is likely that they ultimately led to the breeding of the Irish Draught.

The gentry imported and bred horses solely for racing. Their kind of races were 'Matches' involving only two horses, and took place when two owners wanted to establish whose horse was capable of the greatest speed. Thus they were not merely a pleasant sport, they already involved considerable sums of money.

One of the most famous races of the time was that which was held in 1751 between Bajazet and Black and All Black. The favourite was Bajazet by the Godolphin Arabian, owned by the English Earl of March. Black and All Black also came originally from England but belonged to Sir Ralph Gore, an Irishman. The prize was 1000 guineas, an enormous amount for that time. Furthermore a total of about 10,000 guineas had been placed in bets. The distance of the race was four miles. To prevent his jockey from being bribed, Sir Ralph appointed half a dozen jockeys for the race and only let them know just before the start which of them was to be Black and All Black's rider. The jockey of the Englishman's horse was lighter and to equalize the weight had to wear a belt weighted with lead. In the course of the race, he rid himself of the lead and after the finish had it replaced. This trick, however, did not pass unnoticed; Sir Ralph challenged the Earl of March to a duel on the following morning. Both turned up at the appointed place, but the Earl chose to apologize for what had happened. Sir Ralph accepted his apology and the duel never took place.

As time passed, racing acquired some regulations and became more civilized. In 1727 the first attempts were made to gather and publish the results of the various races held in England. In 1741 John Cheny began covering the racing in Ireland as well as England in his calendar. Cheny died in 1751, but his publication (in which, incidentally, he also reported on cock-fighting) was continued. From then on, however, Irish racing results were published separately.

Up to the mid-eighteenth century, racing in Ireland had been almost exclusively on the flat. Around this time, however, fences were introduced and steeplechasing slowly evolved as a form of racing which was to become such an important part of the whole racing industry in England and Ireland. Steeplechasing, and indeed show-jumping too, evolved from the so-called 'Pounding Matches' which were very popular at that time. Two riders would arrange to meet somewhere out in the countryside, and each in turn point out fences to be cleared. This would continue until one of them gave up. Bets were placed on which horse could keep going the longer.

Tradition has it that the first actual steeplechase took place in 1752 in County Cork. Messrs O'Callaghan and Blake arranged to race from the church in Buttevant across the countryside to Doneraile where the church steeple was to be the winning post. (Hence, it is believed, comes the word 'steeplechase'.) Blake rode a mare called Pam Be Civil and O'Callaghan a stallion Johnny Lad. The race, which covered a distance of four miles, was won by the mare by a length.

Around the same time, special races for hunters were beginning to be held here and there in the country. The actual races were probably on the flat, but to qualify to take part in them, a rider had to show that his horse could jump certain fences. For example, in 1775 a horse had to be able to clear a limestone wall of about 4' 4" and a ditch of about 9' 9" wide, carrying eleven stone, before being considered eligible to run in a hunter race of more than four miles. During one such qualifying test in Loughrea in 1776, Wallach, owned by Mr Richard Darny, is said to have jumped a wall of 7' 2". Bets of up to £400 were placed on the event.

As time passed, race-meetings throughout Ireland began to follow a more or less uniform pattern. Recognized meetings lasted from one day to a week. Up to four races could be held daily, and it was not uncommon for a horse to run not only on two consecutive days, but twice or even three times in the one day. Distances varied from two to four miles. Although most of these races were run on the flat, accidents were not infrequent. In 1752 it was reported that horses were killed after collisions in races at Trim and Loughrea.

At about this time the Jockey Club was established in England. For a while, racing in Ireland came under its jurisdiction until, in 1790, its Irish equivalent, the Irish Turf Club, came into being. Since then, the Irish Turf Club has brought out a racing calendar which contains all regulations for the Turf, and which, up to 1819, did likewise for cock-fighting.

The year 1790 is also important for other reasons. For the first time jumping became part of the actual race and not merely a qualifying test. In this year also, the first handicap race took place.

However, many factors were not yet strictly regulated and loopholes still existed in the rules whereby unusual events could lead to some dispute. One such incident occurred in Ballyshannon in 1792: a certain horse had only a small amount of weight to carry and so was ridden by a young boy. One fence caused the youthful rider to lose his nerve; he dismounted and allowed the horse to clear the wall riderless. He remounted on the other side and came home first. He was disqualified but later the objection was overruled – it seems that the judges discovered that the boy was so light that it would hardly have made any difference whether he had ridden the horse over the wall or not. The saddle would have been sufficient.

Another report, this time from 1819, further illustrates the rather colourful nature of racing at that time. One particular steeplechase had a field of six horses. The course, already rather ambitious, had been made even more difficult by frosty conditions. The result was twelve falls – the winner alone fell four times, the horse in third place six times. Bets had been made as to how many falls there would be. The reporter found it surprising that nobody had been killed. He remarked laconically that steeple-chasing was a sport for which Paddies were famous.

Today English and Irish steeplechasing courses are still the most difficult and taxing.

Flat racing was somewhat less dangerous, but no less strenuous. Before the invention of horse-boxes, horses were ridden to the meetings in which they were to run. They therefore needed less training to keep fit. Munster Lass, a successful mare, winner of eighteen races had, for example, the following programme in one single season: in April she won two four-mile races at one meeting in the Curragh; in June she was a winner in North Antrim and in mid-July at The Maze; seventeen days later she won on two consecutive days at Bellewstown; she had another success in August at Baltinglass, and finished the season with a win in Boyle in September. All in all, she must have covered over 500 miles travelling to these meetings.

Ireland was relatively unaffected by the Napoleonic wars of the late eighteenth and early nineteenth centuries. Agriculture and horse-racing both flourished, as Ireland had an extensive export market for her agricultural products and her horses. The people took little notice of the rumblings of war from the continent and seemed more enthusiastic than ever about racing. Ballad-singers, the news carriers of the time, sang of horses and races – albeit with certain political undertones.

After the Congress of Vienna in 1815, England emerged as one of the leading commercial powers of Europe, owing mainly to the growth of industry at home and of her colonies abroad. The overall standard of living rose sharply, which turned out to be of great benefit to racing. It was becoming an industry in its own right, strengthened by the intensive competition involved. Ireland, however, could not keep up with this rapid development; the people were poor, and active participation in racing had become limited to those individuals who could afford it. Nor could the betting business flourish, as the population on the whole lacked the ready money. Nevertheless, the general enthusiasm did not wane. On the contrary, there are reports of incidents when the onlookers at races became so involved that they attempted to change the official course of the race by building fences of their own.

England set the pace of the racing industry of the time, but Ireland was soon able to adjust its own accordingly. The culmination of this period of development was the establishment of the Aintree Grand National in 1839 and the Irish Derby in 1886.

The Irish Derby was first run because racing was suffering from an economic crisis, and needed a boost. Thirty-eight horses were entered for the first Derby, but in the end there were only four runners.

Participation in this race continued to be bad in the following years. Funds were scarce and to begin with the Derby did not get the recognition it deserved.

The situation improved towards the end of the nineteenth century, in fact the whole racing scene changed its image. 'Match' races between two horses were discontinued, distances were shorter, the average age of race-horses was lowered and speed rather than endurance became more important.

The opening of a number of racecourses near Dublin (Leopardstown in 1888 and the Phoenix Park in 1902) improved the whole racing industry in Ireland to such an extent that in 1907, an Irish-trained horse won the Epsom Derby for the first time. The horse Orby was also the first Catholic-owned horse to win this race.

Around this time the other Irish classic races were established. In 1895 the Oaks was run for the first time, in 1916 the St Leger and in 1921 and 1922 the 2000 and 1000 guineas respectively. Since then they have been held at the Curragh.

The Irish Derby finally came into its own in the years following the First World War, when a number of English horses were entered for it each year. Between the years 1919 and 1939 the English were winners fourteen times.

The Irish Derby of 1925 saw the first of five victories for the Aga Khan's horses. This series of successes is indicative of the influence he has had on thoroughbred sport in Ireland since then.

Indeed, 1925 was the highest point of the inter-war years. After that, the levying of entertainment tax on entrance fees and betting caused the racing industry to struggle for existence. A further reason for its decline was a dispute with the British government which demanded a

40 per cent tax on horses imported from Ireland. One positive move, however, was the introduction of the Totalisator in 1930, which improved the financial circumstances of thoroughbred sports. The crisis seemed to be nearing its end by the outbreak of the Second World War.

The experience gained by these setbacks, particularly the financial ones, led to the setting up of the Racing Board in 1945, an association which, since then, has assessed the financial situation of racing, and if necessary, aided it. This proved to be beneficial to the industry and is still instrumental in its maintenance. The move to establish the Board was mainly due to the efforts of Joseph McGrath, a well-known breeder and owner of the time.

So began the modern racing era. The upward trend was partly due to the involvement of a number of American owners in the industry, but the influence of certain individual trainers must also be acknowledged, the exceptional genius of two men in particular.

Before the war, P. J. Prendergast was a steeplechase jockey. During the war he tried to join the RAF, but before he could do so he was imprisoned by the Special Branch in Liverpool for suspected membership of the IRA, and was duly sent back to Ireland. A few months later in a bar he met an owner looking for a trainer. Prendergast applied for a trainer's licence and took two horses into his care. After a short while he had his first successes and it soon became evident that he had a special talent for the training of two-year-olds. In 1950 he produced his first two-year-old to become champion, a feat which he repeated no less than twelve times between then and 1965. In the same year he had his first classic wins (the 1000 Guineas and the Irish Derby) and to date he has had twenty classic winners. He was the first trainer to win the Irish Derby twice and in 1965 was claimed champion trainer in England three times in succession – a rare honour.

The outstanding feature of his method of training is his apparent reliance on instinct when dealing with a horse.

Vincent O'Brien, on the other hand, is a trainer of more studied, intellectual methods, who, right from the beginning, sets out to achieve a definite objective. His father was a farmer who also trained horses with remarkable success. After his father's death, Vincent rented from his step-brother the few buildings and land in Cork which comprised their farm and in 1944 took out a licence as a public trainer.

He began his career as a trainer with three horses – his own, a rented one and another. From the outset, he was extraordinarily successful – in both steeplechasing and flat-racing. In the early years, he made his name as a trainer of steeplechasers, not because he necessarily specialized in this field, but because he trained what was given to him. In 1949 he won his first Cheltenham Gold Cup, a victory which he later repeated twice. He won the Grand National in 1953, 1954 and 1955, and finally in 1957 he gave up training steeplechasers, having won all the prizes worth taking in this field.

In the meantime, he had left Churchtown and had moved his ever-growing stables to Ballydoyle in County Tipperary. While looking for new premises for his training grounds he consulted some of his older colleagues. They advised him not to set up in the Curragh as conditions there were too uniform for a varied training. O'Brien must have recognized the potential of his present premises right from the start – even though they are not particularly special at first glance. Over the years he has set out his training grounds so expertly that they now afford conditions for training that are among the best in existence. His track, for example, has been laid out in strips, one with cinders, one with wood shavings, one with turf, etc. – so that horses can gallop on them all year round and training can continue whatever the weather.

Despite the successes abroad, particularly those of these two trainers, racing in Ireland had little international significance up to 1960. Irish trainers, riders and horses were good enough to win the most important races abroad; few horses from abroad, on the other hand, came to race in Ireland, as prize money was not sufficiently high in Irish races to attract foreign entries.

Attempts were made to change this situation towards the end of the fifties. It was clear to everyone involved what the actual problem was; but only one man came up with what should be done. Money was needed. Once again, it was Joseph McGrath, founder of the Racing Board, who thought up a scheme. At that time, he was president of the Irish Hospitals' Sweepstakes, an organization which ran lotteries on horse-races in aid of Irish hospitals. He planned to widen this organization and incorporated the Irish Derby into it.

A short look at the history of this unique organization at this point might help to explain its method of operation. In medieval times, in Ireland as elsewhere, medical care of the people lay in the hands of the monasteries or of charitable institutions endowed by private funds. As the influence of the Reformation spread during the reign of Henry VIII, the monasteries were closed down and, to a great extent, the people were left without any institutionalized medical centres. Ironically, Henry VIII was a generous patron of horse-racing – but unfortunately in those days the welfare of the hospital system had nothing to do with racing, as it has today. It is interesting to note that as early as 1745, a hospital was built by private endowment, the building costs of which were largely covered by the profits made by holding a lottery. On the whole, though, the financial circumstances of the medical service were very bad, and right up to the 1920s, little funding came from government sources.

In 1930, the representative committees of six Dublin hospitals decided to take the task of fund-raising into their own hands, and proceeded to organize a lottery based on the results of certain races. This they called the Sweepstake. The ingenuity and subsequent success of their scheme lay in the fact that, while fulfilling a much-needed charitable function, it also appealed to two basic passions of the Irish – gambling and horse-racing.

The first Sweepstake made over £130,000 for the six hospitals which initiated it. The second made £440,000 for what was now twenty-three hospitals, and the third just under £700,000 to be divided among thirty-four hospitals. The whole organization had progressed to such an extent that during the Second World War, Ireland was able to subsidize the work of the Red Cross, and to finance the building and staffing of a hospital in France.

With the incorporation of the Irish Derby into the scheme in 1962, Irish hospitals and the racing industry were affiliated more closely, with a considerably larger financial profit for both. The Irish Derby, in existence since 1866, now became the Sweeps Derby. To attract international interest, the Hospital Trust contributed £30,000 in prize money – the greatest amount which a single sponsor has ever endowed a race. In 1977, with £100,966.50 in prize money, the Irish Sweeps Derby is among the richest races in the world. As a result it attracts a very considerable entry.

The hospitals, as partners in this arrangement, have benefited by revenue in excess of £100 million.

For this reason, the financial circumstances of Irish racing are not bad, despite the economic recession. Admittedly they still cannot be compared with those enjoyed by the racing industry in France.

Those in the racing industry have high hopes for the quality of future racehorses. The present preponderance of American horses does not seem to bother the Irish. They know from experience that single breeding lines often dominate for a few years, and then are replaced by others. In the thirties, for example, English racing was to the fore; in the fifties, the French, and now American. The significance of this fact is not looked on as alarming in any way, because American racing has evolved in a completely different tradition to European racing. Each form of racing is a different type of sport – which makes it difficult to compare performances on both sides of the Atlantic. It is like the case of soccer and rugby: both are ball games but other than that they have little in common.

Racing in Europe is usually over classic distances of one mile to one and three-quarter miles. Seventy per cent of the money placed in bets (winner or place) goes on these races. The remaining 30 per cent is placed on the shorter races. American races are primarily of the latter type. This, therefore, leaves a relatively wide scope for the Irish who prefer stayers to sprinters.

Ireland will continue to hold a high place among the racing nations of the world, on the one hand because racing in Ireland is backed by a strong breeding industry, and on the other hand because the Irish have emerged as a seasoned racing people who will always manage to find a way around whatever difficulties or problems arise.

The racecourse at Laytown, Co. Meath, about thirty-five miles north of Dublin, has a most unusual track; races there are held on the strand. However they have come to be more a tourist attraction than genuine sporting events, and are held only in summer, during the tourist season

3

Show-jumping

Supreme mastery

A heavy stone wall was the first occurrence of note. Flurry chose a place where the top was loose, and his clumsy-looking brown mare changed feet on the rattling stones like a fairy. Sorcerer came at it tense and collected as a bow at full stretch, and sailed steeply into the air; I saw the wall far beneath me, with an unsuspected ditch on the far side, and I felt my hat following me at the full stretch of its guard as we swept over it, then, with a long slant, we descended to earth some sixteen feet from where we had left it, and I was possessor of the gratifying fact that I had achieved a good-sized 'fly', and had not perceptibly moved in my saddle. Subsequent disillusioning experience has taught me that but few horses jump like Sorcerer, so gallantly, so sympathetically, and with such supreme mastery of the subject; but none the less the enthusiasm that he imparted to me has never been extinguished . . .*

* From Somerville and Ross, see Note, p. 187.

In 1864, at the first Horse Show of the Royal Dublin Society, a competition was held which offered prizes to those horses which proved to be most suitable for hunting. They were in the form of simple tests of jumping, but were in fact the first show-jumping events not only in Ireland but in the world. It is not surprising that show-jumping should have begun in Ireland, considering the ideal conditions which exist there. From this first show of the Royal Dublin Society, the present Dublin Horse Show has evolved over the years, and, as then, is still run by the same society.

The Royal Dublin Society (RDS) was founded in 1731, but only in later years had it anything to do with the business of horse-breeding. It was founded by private initiative. A group of progressive Irishmen felt that the English Government was not doing all it could for Ireland. At first, their main objective was to sponsor the development of agriculture; later they became active in the areas of crafts, science and the arts. In this way the society has contributed a great deal to the general improvement of life in Ireland. It also provided the necessary boost to equestrian sport and breeding. The society's decision to involve itself in these two areas was taken in 1861. In the beginning it organized two small horse shows as experiments.

When these proved successful, it was decided, in 1868 to hold shows annually. Right from the start, horses were judged not only by their appearance but also by their performance. For this latter purpose 'high' and 'wide' jumping tests were devised. In both, only one fence had to be cleared, and the criteria for judging a horse remained entirely at the discretion of the judges. The fence for the high jump usually consisted of three horizontal bars decorated with gorse; unfortunately no details exist as to the height of these fences. The wide jump was made up of a number of hurdles placed next to each other; further than this we know nothing of these jumps, either. The winners in these two competitions received five pounds each, and those in second place two pounds each, fairly generous prizes for the time.

Previous page: Inis Cara ridden by Larry Kiely

A further jump was included in the test; this time over a stone wall, a jump to which, it seems, considerable importance was attached, since its prizes were greater. The first prize was a cup worth about ten pounds, and the second a whip valued at about five pounds. It is interesting to note that to qualify for this competition, a horse had to be able to jump a wooden fence of approximately four and a half feet.

These tests, the forerunners of modern show-jumping, were repeated the following year. They apparently attracted widespread interest for the prizes were doubled. In 1870 more definite judging criteria were laid down – the judge's decision was to be made on the form and style which the rider demonstrated. The fences were also changed: a water-filled ditch ten feet in width became the wide jump, not unlike the water-jump used today.

As we have already mentioned, it is not surprising that show-jumping should have originated in Ireland. In the first place, hunting required a horse which could jump, and the countryside in Ireland through which the hunt passed would present a wider variety of natural fences than most other places. The people needed a practical opportunity to test the jumping ability and general skill of a horse designated for the hunt. Secondly, the general passion for competitive sports must have been instrumental in the instigation and subsequent success of these jumping competitions.

Just as the so-called 'pounding matches' referred to in the chapter on racing would have been the sources from which both show-jumping and steeplechasing evolved, so could the horses entered for the matches be said to be the ancestors of both show-jumpers and steeplechasers.

To return to the history of the Royal Dublin Society Horse Show – in 1881 jumping events for both horses and ponies were held, much on the same lines as those of today. The riders had now to contend with not one but various fences set out in a prescribed order. This first course comprised a bank, a stone wall, a water-jump and hurdles. The horse had to carry a stipulated minimum weight. In 1895 jumping events were held at the RDS Spring Show as well as at the usual show in autumn. It is also worth mentioning that approximately half the competitions then were open only to four-year-olds. This is indicative of the nature of these competitions – they were still first and foremost a means of evaluating the ability of future hunters, and not yet competitions in themselves. One event per year was reserved for ladies' hunters – but only men were allowed to participate in the competition!

The small town of Ballymena in the north of Ireland emerged as an important show-jumping centre, not only as the venue of numerous trials, but also as the home of many successful riders and horses. However, the number of actual show-jumping riders was relatively small, because already the ranks were confined to professionals. For example, it was reported that of the twenty-seven entries in a show-jumping event in Belfast, twelve were ridden by Sam Bailie and eleven by Alec Rodgers.

Strangely enough, the regulations for these trials did not include any criteria for judging. The judges made decisions in accordance with their own preferences – a fact which gave rise to some rather amusing incidents. It is related, for example, that one horse was disqualified because the judges felt that an animal with such a bad mouth would never make a decent hunter. Whatever one's reaction to that opinion might be, the following certainly would give rise to question: one lady wanted to know why her horse had been so badly placed. The judge replied that although the horse had jumped quite well, he hadn't particularly liked its rider's hat!

The time element had not yet been included in the regulations for show-jumping. Therefore the pace of these competitions was probably quite leisurely.

Show-jumping in those days was not a money-making undertaking. The total sum given in prizes was often less than that made on entry fees. Once again, it was thanks to the general public's interest that show-jumping survived. It was new, but the enthusiasm and support of the people caused it not only to survive, but to grow and flourish. Even during the First World War, when the Dublin Horse Show was not held, show-jumping events in the country continued to be as popular as ever.

The 1921 Horse Show first introduced a scoring system – a plus-point system unlike that of today. Points were scored for a good performance and not for faults.

One of the most significant years in the history of Irish show-jumping was 1926, which marked the beginning of the era of international show-jumping. The initiator was not Irish, but Swiss. At that time the Swiss army bought between 500 and 1000 Irish horses each year. Indeed, Irish animals made up the largest contingent of Swiss army horses, and until shortly after the end of the First World War virtually no competition was offered by other countries. The situation changed when other horse-breeding countries such as Germany, France and Poland began to get over the after-effects of the war. In 1925 two Swiss colonels, Ziegler and Haccius, who were responsible for the buying of new mounts suggested that the Irish set up some international show-jumping competitions and participate in them themselves. In this way they would have the opportunity to demonstrate the quality of Irish horses and to attract prospective breeders. The following year the RDS carried out this suggestion: the first Nations Cup competition took place in Ballsbridge. Ironically, the Swiss won first prize.

In order to form Irish equestrian teams for taking part in events abroad, efforts were made to found an army riding school, whose primary function would be the training of officers for show-jumping. They, in turn, would attract foreign interest in Irish horses. This riding school, therefore, has never had any military significance. Its first team of officers was made up of successful point-to-point and hunt riders. From 1928 new recruits were instructed and trained by Paul Rodzianko, a former Russian cavalry officer. Before the First World War he had ridden for Russia and had been trained in various European cavalry schools. He worked in the Italian cavalry school Pinerolo, under Caprilli, founder of the modern jumping style. The practice of appointing foreign trainers continued, as it was felt that they would make Irish riders more conversant with Continental standards.

The importance of creating a top-class riding team was recognized by the Minister for Agriculture, Patrick Hogan, who encouraged and subsidized the undertaking. After a few years, the first team had achieved a standard

In Ireland show-jumping is very much part of a day's work. Jumping competitions provide a number of opportunities: to test what a horse has learnt, to win money, and to have at one's disposal a ready-made market for the buying and selling of horses. For this reason, the atmosphere in the jumping enclosure in Ireland is more professional, less complicated than in other countries and, for the Irish horseman, part of his everyday life

Until recently Ireland has to a large extent been represented by army officers at show-jumping events abroad. The training centre for Irish officers and certain civilians is at McKee Barracks in the Phoenix Park, Dublin. Here members of the army who have shown promise while cadets at the Curragh Camp go through their training

at least equal to that of any other European team. This was the result of the intensive training schemes for which Rodzianko was famous. According to his pupils, their training was very tough – work came before anything else.

The years between 1930 and 1939 were the most successful in the history of Irish show-jumping. Only in individual cases has such a high standard of performance been shown since. With their successes in the year 1936, the Irish established themselves as first-class show-jumpers: in that season they won nine team and twenty-five individual events. Victories such as John Lewis's winning of the Irish Cup in London in 1934, have not been repeated since. It is said that after his victory, the band tried to play the Irish National Anthem but did not know it. An Irishman among the spectators whistled the melody for them and the musicians managed to repeat it.

Judging by their achievements during those years, the Irish team in all probability would have been successful at the Berlin Olympic Games, but on political grounds they did not participate. The fact that the German team, Olympic champions at Berlin, were beaten by the Irish team in the following year at the Nations Prize in Aachen, further suggests this.

After the Second World War, during which the army riding school was suspended, both the school and show-jumping in general were reorganized. Until 1949 international competitions were open only to military teams, but since then civilians have also participated.

At the same time show-jumping finally evolved as a sport in its own right; its connection with hunting which, until then had been maintained, was finally severed. However, fences similar to those encountered on the hunt in Ireland, were still included in courses for international events – fences such as single and double banks, water-jumps and walls. At first these courses were designed in the way they had always been for show-jumping events in Ireland, but once the RDS joined FEI (Fédération Equestre Internationale), general FEI standards were somewhat reluctantly adopted. The FEI had some difficulty in seeing that their requirements were carried out, because for a long time the Irish continued to judge a jumping fault in terms of its possible consequences on the hunt. For example, a fault with the forelegs on the hunt would be likely to cause a fall and be much more dangerous than touching a fence with the hind-legs. Landing in the middle of a natural water-filled ditch could have serious consequences whereas merely putting a foot into the water at the edge would hardly matter at all. Banks should be jumped cleanly – not scrambled up on one side and slid down on the other. A single bank should be negotiated with two jumps – one on to it and one off it – while a double bank has space on top of it for one gallop stride before jumping off it again. However, as show-jumping became separated from hunting, Ireland finally took on FEI standards in 1951. Interestingly enough, jumping against the clock was not introduced in Ireland until 1938, whereas it had been a feature of show-jumping on the Continent many years before that, mainly on account of its spectacular nature.

In the mid-fifties, the modern era of show-jumping began. Rising standards of living made it possible for more people to own horses and take part in competitions. At the same time show-jumping was also becoming popular as a spectator sport, and certain commercial companies began to use horses as a means of advertising. Show-jumping was becoming a professional sport.

The prices paid for potential top-class jumpers began to rise, and Ireland, owing to the first-class quality of her horses, became the centre of the market. Horses showing great promise attracted increasing numbers of foreign buyers. As a result, the chances of victory for Irish riders in international competitions rapidly dwindled. However, their chances improved when in 1963 the first Irish team of military and civilian riders took part in international contests. This team had four horses which were among the best ever to be produced in Ireland: Dundrum, ridden by Tommy Wade; Goodbye, ridden by Seamus Hayes; Barrymore, ridden by Diana Conolly-Carew, and Loch an Easpaigh, ridden by Captain Ringrose.

Although by now civilian riders were taking part in international events, the best training for riders and horses was still available only to military personnel at the army riding school. This training centre is situated at

McKee Barracks in the Phoenix Park, Dublin. To a large extent, instructors there have been foreigners: Colonel Rodzianko was followed – for periods of different lengths – by Jed O'Dwyer (who used Rodzianko's methods), Major Kulesza from Poland, John Lewis, Seamus Hayes and Jock Ferrie, an Englishman.

The training centre remained at McKee Barracks even after the setting up of Bórd na gCapall (the Irish Horse Board), whose function is the development of all branches of the non-thoroughbred industry. (Bórd na gCapall was established by the Government in 1970. Its role in equestrian sport in Ireland will be dealt with in greater detail in a later chapter.) Since 1968 eventing has also been added to the activities of the training centre at the barracks in the Phoenix Park – the first Three-day Event horse was presented to the army by Sir John Galvin, a well-known patron of the sport.

Bórd na gCapall's first trainer for both army and civilian riders was Colonel Zgorzelsky, originally from Poland. With his help, Antony Paalman, a Dutchman, built up the present group of internationally successful riders. Paalman worked for the Show Jumping Association where he had particular responsibility for the training and general welfare of young riders. Both these experts worked in Ireland until 1972, when their work was taken over by Erich Bubbel, who remained in the position until 1977. Bubbel, formerly a Prussian cavalry officer, made a name for himself in the past as trainer of Sir John Galvin's successful event horses in America.

These men were all official trainers in equestrian institutions, but the contribution of a certain lady on a private basis is no less important. The lady in question is Iris Kellet, a one-time European champion. When she retired from active sport, she set up a riding school in Dublin, where riders and horses were trained to international level. Her most famous pupil is Eddie Macken. Recently she sold her school in Dublin, and had new first-class premises built in Kill, County Kildare. These fine new quarters merely provide the background to the real source of these young riders' successes – Iris Kellett's subtle and skilful training methods.

The principal aim of show-jumping in Ireland is, as it always has been, the training of show-jumpers and the attracting of buyers. This very definite aim makes it different from show-jumping in other countries, where it is a sport for its own sake. This aspect is evident in show-jumping throughout Ireland – both on a regional and international level. The small, local jumping competitions, for example, are held in association with agricultural shows, a state of affairs which often lends a most entertaining atmosphere to the whole proceedings.

In most cases, the results of these competitions are decided upon after one round of jumps, as jump-offs are not common with young horses. Because time is not taken into consideration, riders with the same amount of points share the victory or place in the ranking – a solution which suits everyone.

Jumping competitions of 'Grade B' category are only open to horses with total winnings of under £300. Prizes for competitions in this category are up to £25.

Grade A competitions – the more important national and international competitions – are for horses with total winnings of more than £300. Prizes for these range from £30 to £100. Three-day Event competitions are not so well endowed. Except in international events in this class, where £100 to £200 can be won, prizes are usually between £10 and £20.

Smaller jumping events or shows are usually held on weekdays. For most of those taking part they are part of a day's work, not a leisure pursuit as is the case in other countries. On the one hand, they provide an opportunity to put a horse through its paces and win money, and on the other hand, they provide a market for the buying and selling of horses. Irish horse-dealers are always present at the jumping grounds, and often agents for foreign buyers too. They bargain and negotiate, and at the same time take note of the development in the careers of certain horses.

The objective of international show-jumping in Ireland is almost exclusively the sale of horses. The fact that a large number of Irish horses have made their name in other countries, ridden by foreign riders, does not necessarily mean that the Irish do not recognize their potential or that Irish riders were not good enough. It means that Ireland is not rich enough to afford the luxury of show-jumping as the prestige sport it tends to be elsewhere. The Irish make their living by selling their horses. Nevertheless, a sufficient number of horses are kept at home to form an efficient riding team. They, for their part, provide an advertisement for the Irish horse-breeding industry, one of the most important industries in the country.

This frame of mind might seem strange and callous to people from other countries. For the Irish, however, it is one of the facts of life. It was evident recently, for example, when Eddie Macken, one of Ireland's most promising young riders, emigrated to Germany. Nobody seemed to mind terribly that he was lost to Irish show-jumping: people saw that in a practical way he could do as much good for Irish horses in Germany as he could at home.

Irish show-jumping, in being so closely associated with the breeding industry, is fulfilling a function every bit as gratifying and important as the achievement of successes in the sporting world. The breeding of top-class horses is as necessary as their training for successful sporting careers.

Right: Moet et Chandon (out of Morning Light) ridden by Hubert Parot (France)

The Hunt

A man who knows his horse

Up the road a hound gave a yelp of discovery, and flung himself over a stile into the fields; the rest of the pack went squealing and jostling after him, and I followed Flurry over one of those infinitely varied erections pleasantly termed 'gaps' in Ireland. On this occasion the gap was made of three razor-edged slabs of slate leaning against an iron bar, and Sorcerer conveyed to me his thorough knowledge of the matter by a lift of his hindquarters that made me feel as if I were being skilfully kicked downstairs. To what extent I looked it, I cannot say . . . I only know that undeserved good luck restored to me my stirrup before Sorcerer got away with me in the next field.

What followed was, I am told, a very fast fifteen minutes; for me time was not; the empty fields rushed past uncounted, fences came and went in a flash, while the wind sang in my ears, and the dazzle of the early sun was in my eyes. I saw the hounds occasionally, sometimes pouring over a green bank, as the charging breaker lifts and flings itself, sometimes driving across a field, as the white tongues of foam slide racing over the sand; and always ahead of me was Flurry Knox, going as a man goes who knows his country, who knows his horse, and whose heart is wholly and absolutely in the right place.*

* From Somerville and Ross, see Note, p. 187.

The importance of the hunt in Ireland and the fame it has gained for the country are due to the suitability of the Irish countryside, in all its variations, for hunting. Riders from other countries can only dream of such conditions. The topographical variations in Ireland mean that conditions for hunting vary from county to county. Different styles of hunting have developed in accordance with the nature of the terrain in the various regions. The name of the hunt in each region is therefore often associated with certain characteristics.

For example, the famous Galway Blazers hunt in the barren landscape of the West of Ireland. They ride at high speed over the numerous stone walls which are characteristic of that area. Experts say that nowhere else in the world offers such good conditions for the hunt. The Galway Blazers have a reputation for recklessness – it is said that a group of riders from Galway once revelled so boisterously in a certain hotel that it finally burst into flames, an event which, some say, gave the group their name. Other more reputable sources, claim that the name originates from one of their foremost riders who had a particularly remarkable mop of red hair.

A pack in County Tipperary is known as the Scarteen Black and Tans, so called because of the colour of the hounds. The countryside there is more mellow and offers a different type of obstacle to clear – immense, often double, banks, ditches and hedges – all of which are best taken at a slower pace. Similar conditions exist in Meath, Limerick and Dublin.

A different type of horse is used in each of these regions. In Galway hunters are lighter, usually of thoroughbred or Connemara pony ancestry. In Limerick and Tipperary, middle- and heavyweight hunters are preferred. The more easy-going nature of these horses lessens the likelihood of falling into a ditch.

Not only the horses are bred especially for the hunt. The history of hound-breeding is equally traditional. As early as the beginning of the eighteenth century, special faster horses were bred for hunting, but the specialized breeding of hounds only dates from the nineteenth century, when huntsmen discovered that the hounds were having some difficulty in keeping in front of the horses.

The history of Irish hounds is interwoven with legend. Some say, for example, that the Kerry beagles are descended from the hounds of St Hubert, patron saint of the hunt. The claim that hounds in Ireland today are descendants of the dogs which swam ashore after the sinking of the Spanish Armada off the west coast of Ireland is even less credible. The same story, incidentally, is told, equally falsely, of the origin of the Connemara ponies. Somewhat more authentic is the claim that Brian Boru, King of Ireland in the eleventh century kept dogs which he used for hunting. The lineage of the oldest pack in existence today goes back more than two hundred years.

Hugo Meynell, an Englishman, a famous breeder of hounds, was responsible for originating the present-day breed of foxhound. The man who succeeded Meynell as Master of the Quorn pack, further developed the fast style of hunting to such an extent that he used to take extra horses with him on the hunt so as to be able to keep up the same pace all day. The partiality for fast hunting was so strong in some that they used to race with each other while on the hunt (which led to the beginnings of steeplechasing: in its early days it almost exclusively involved huntsmen).

The hunt provides an excellent opportunity to train young jumpers and event horses. A young horse could hardly receive a better preliminary training than to be set to gallop with more experienced horses and to have to find the best ways of getting over fences of every kind. On the one hand, skills and a sense of awareness and determination are developed, and on the other, it gives an opportunity for trainers to single out particularly talented horses which would warrant further training. It is here that Irish horses acquire independence, one of their most fundamental characteristics.

The hunt not only offers a splendid training for young horses, but can also provide a welcome change for the overtaxed 'professionals' who need something to re-awaken their desire to jump. These horses, like the young horses who show potential for top-class performance, are only allowed to join easier hunts on account of the high incidence of injury. Cub-hunts, for example, which train

Master, huntsmen and hounds by the Rock of Cashel in Co. Tipperary. Horse and man have grown up with this traditional sport; everything which makes up the hunt has been part of them since their earliest youth

young hounds for their future fox-hunting careers are less demanding.

Beagling helps to train young riders for the hunt, and as such is worth mentioning. Future huntsmen can get to know the treacherous parts of the countryside on foot and experience for themselves the difficulties which a horse might encounter.

But we must return to the main aspect of hunting – its role as a traditional leisure activity. Late in the morning the huntsmen meet and after one or two whiskeys, they ride forth with the pack, undeterred by any obstacle which might stand in their way. Even the most seasoned horseman from the Continent can lose his nerve coming up to an Irish ditch, so deep that he dare not look down when jumping it, and from which he would not be able to climb out without help should he fall in; or when facing a hedge or wall not knowing what is behind. If you were to ask him how he managed it once he was on the other side, you'd be likely to get the answer '*I'm* over it, thank goodness! That's all I know.'

The Irish hunt tears through hedges full of thorns; rides dauntlessly across main roads, if the hounds have gone that way. Few obstacles are impossible to jump or clear somehow or other. Hunting is the greatest source of pleasure for the Irish; they are passionately addicted to it from November to March.

Hunters are seldom used outside the hunting season. Usually they are left to graze throughout the summer. Nobody bothers much about them until autumn, when they are brought in and put through a short period of training to make them fit again. They will ride with the hunt twice or three times a week throughout the season, most of which will be run at full gallop. Sometimes the quarry – stag, fox or hare – will be hunted down quickly by the hounds, in which case the hunt could be over in as little as one or two hours. However, it is more likely to last much longer and not to end until two or three foxes have been killed.

Often the chase lasts from morning to twilight, during which time the horses gallop at full tilt over the fields. In the long run it depends on the rider whether the whole exercise is too much for the horse. An experienced horse who knows the ins and outs of the terrain and who knows what to expect will not, on the whole, find hunting too difficult. In the case of a young, inexperienced horse, however, the rider will try to take the easiest way and not hesitate to drop out of the hunt if his horse is overtired. This is the essence of 'horsemanship' – that quality which refers to a rider's understanding of and sensitivity towards his horse, a quality which is innate in so many Irishmen. If, on the other hand, a rider should withdraw from the hunt just because he has come off his horse (and is not injured, of course), or is soaked to the skin, or maybe scratched all over by thorns, he would have to have a very thick skin indeed to be able to face the other huntsmen later in the evening when they all gather round the fire.

There are three different kinds of horseback hunting in Ireland today – hunting for foxes, hares and stags. At the moment thirty-seven registered foxhunting packs are kept throughout the country, the average size of a pack being twenty couples. Most of these packs have been owned by certain families for generations and are bred with tradition in mind. The keeper of the pack bears the coveted title of Master of Hounds. Occasionally some of these animals are exported, usually to America, Australia or New Zealand.

There are thirty registered packs of harriers in Ireland. The size of a harrier pack is usually smaller than that of foxhounds.

Only two packs exist for hunting deer – so-called Staghounds; one of these is kept in County Meath, the other in Northern Ireland.

Foxes and hares are usually chased and hunted in their natural surroundings in the open countryside. Deer, on the other hand are kept in parks and, for the purposes of hunting, are let loose in a suitable terrain. When one is cornered by the hounds, it is simply recaptured – not killed – and returned to the park where it is left in peace until the next hunt.

In the past few years hunting has been badly affected by the introduction of modern farming methods and more intensive land-utilization. Riding through the countryside – an activity long since impossible in most European countries – is becoming more difficult even in Ireland.

Areas which used to be uncultivated are now being re-
claimed for agricultural use. New fences – some with
barbed wire – are being built across one-time hunting
terrain, and more and more frequently the path of the
hunt has to be specially mapped out beforehand. Permission has to be acquired from landowners if the hunt is
to pass through their lands; wire on fences has to be
removed beforehand and replaced afterwards.

The ever-growing number of people riding with the
hunt is also causing concern. A group of over fifty horses
leaves its mark on any land it traverses.

Various ways of dealing with these problems have been
suggested. Some people want to limit the size of the hunt,
objecting in particular to the increasing number of
foreigners who now ride to hounds in Ireland. On the
other hand, the contribution of these foreigners to
tourism and other service industries cannot be over-
looked. Nor should it be forgotten that the same
foreigners frequently want to buy the horse they have
ridden on the hunt.

None of these difficulties, however, is of any great
significance. There is little doubt that, with a certain
amount of change and adaptation, Ireland will continue
to offer ideal conditions for hunting.

Breeding

Outraged maternal feeling

Wherever the brown mare came from, I can certify that it was not out of double harness. Though humble and anxious to oblige, she pulled away from the pole as if it were red hot, and at critical moments had a tendency to sit down. However, we squeezed without misadventure among the donkey carts and between the groups of people, and bumped at length in safety out on to the high-road . . .

We had reached the foot of a hill; the Castle Knox horse addressed himself to it with dignified determination, but the mare showed a sudden and alarming tendency to jib.

'Belt her, Major!' vociferated Slipper, as she hung back from the pole chain, with the collar half-way up her ewe-neck, 'and give it to the horse, too! He'll drag her!'

I was in the act of 'belting' when a squealing whinney struck upon my ear, accompanied by a light pattering gallop on the road behind us; there was an answering roar from the brown mare, a roar, as I realized with a sudden-drop of the heart, of outraged maternal feeling, and in another instant a pale, yellow foal sprinted up beside us, with shrill whickerings of joy. Had there at this moment been a bog-hole handy, I should have turned the bus into it without hesitation; as there was no accommodation of the kind, I laid the whip severely into everything I could reach, including the foal. The result was that we topped the hill at a gallop, three abreast, like a Russian troika . . .

There was no sign from my inside passengers, and I held on at a round pace, the mother and child galloping absurdly, the carriage horse pulling hard, but behaving like a gentleman . . . and here the fateful sound of galloping behind us was again heard.

'It's impossible!' I said to myself; 'she can't have twins!'*

* From Somerville and Ross, see Note, p. 187.

It is difficult to define the actual qualities which make Ireland a good place for breeding horses. Experience has simply shown that conditions in Ireland are particularly suitable for horse-breeding, be they geographic, climatic, or as a result of some other factor. Being a relatively small island, Ireland has a moderate climate; the proximity of the sea means that summers are not too hot and that the winters are mild. The Gulf Stream flowing off the west coast of the country has a positive influence on the climate. Frequent rainfall carried by constant winds ensures a relatively high atmospheric humidity, a good growth of grass and not too many troublesome insects. Soil with a high lime content gives the grass many nutrients which are invaluable for young horses growing up.

But it is not only ideal conditions such as these that have helped to put Irish horses among the best in the world. An equally important factor has been the constant selection which has been insisted upon from the start in Ireland, and which, one hopes, will continue in the future. In a relatively poor country such as Ireland, horses are bred for profit. Only the best, therefore, is good enough.

This state of affairs has also helped to make the Irish into experts on all aspects of the breeding and rearing of horses. If you cannot judge the quality of a horse, you do not stand a chance in the business.

All these factors have resulted in the Irish producing the best, whatever the area of horse-breeding – thoroughbred, chaser or pony.

Thoroughbred Breeding

It has already been mentioned that the breeding of thoroughbreds dates from the publication of the first Studbook in England in 1793. Its first entries were the three Arab stallions, the Byerley Turk, the Darley Arabian and the Godolphin Barb, together with a number of home-bred mares, the so-called Royal Mares, each of which had been specially bred for racing. Among them were some mares of Irish ancestry chosen for their proven quality. The large number of 'Hobbies' – the racehorses of the time – which had been exported to England and the Continent from Ireland speak for the relatively high standards of horse-breeding which must have already existed in Ireland. The Italian Raphael Maffeo Volaterno refers to these horses in his travel memoirs written in the sixteenth century. He claimed that, with the exception of corn and excellent horses, one could find nothing worth mentioning in Ireland. It is interesting to note that in that century Ireland had already begun to export horses, but we do not know whether it was this report of Volaterno that brought the quality of Irish horses to the attention of the Italians. In any case, the main buyers were the Dukes of Ferrara and Modena. They made their purchases through an agent named Blasio de Bivago.

Evidence of other exports can be found in the stud register of the fifth Duke of Northumberland: the entries for 1512 included four Irish Hobbies. From the start, thoroughbred breeding in Britain and Ireland has been closely connected, and thus its history in both countries is very similar. It is interesting and worthwhile, therefore, to examine the ways in which thoroughbred breeding in Ireland differs from that in Britain.

The Byerley Turk was brought to Ireland during a military campaign and is believed to have been later sent to stud there for a while. Some hold, rather maliciously, that, in true soldier fashion, he had simply left descendants behind him. Be that as it may, the fact remains that one way or another, the best blood was in Ireland at the very start of the great age of thoroughbred breeding. This situation did not change in the years following; even then, many English owners preferred to have their horses brought up in Ireland. The east coast was a particularly popular area for breeding.

The racing calendar of 1794 gives some interesting information about breeding at that time. Breeders used it to advertise their stallions, much as they do today. The stud fee for the stallion Tug, for example, was five pounds for thoroughbred mares and half that amount for other mares. Grooms' fees were also required even in those days.

Towards the beginning of the nineteenth century interest in thoroughbred breeding became more widespread. The best blood was now being bred in Galway and Sligo as well as Kildare. In later years these counties were to lose their significance as breeding areas. However, in about 1860, a horse from Galway played an important part in the history of Irish breeding. This was Darling's Day, who had already proved herself an excellent brood mare before being sent by her owner to be covered by West Australian, the only stallion in Ireland at the time to have Matchem blood. However, west Australian had just been sold and was on the point of being exported to France. In fact, when the mare arrived from Galway, the stallion was being taken on board the ship. Fortunately, the mare's long journey from the West was taken into consideration and the mating was allowed to take place. The product was Solon who himself sired many excellent progeny. If his parents had not met in this way at the eleventh hour, there would be no Matchem blood in Ireland now.

Another important event in Irish thoroughbred breeding – though of an entirely different nature – took place in January 1866. In the racing calendar of that year, a Mr Robert Goff offered his services as nominated auctioneer to the Turf Club. Who could have foreseen that that seemingly insignificant advertisement would lead to an organization which was eventually to become the nerve-centre of the breeding and racing industries? It was the start of bloodstock auctioneering in Ireland – the instrument of the thoroughbred market. It had already been proved in England that auctioneering offered the best opportunities for trading in horses. The undertaking grew with continuing success, but always remained slightly overshadowed by auctioneering in England. Nowadays, however, it looks as though the Goff organization might offer serious competition to its British counterpart. This came about as a result of what, at the time, looked like unfavourable circumstances: up to 1973 the company had sold its horses in the RDS grounds, and when these were sold in that year Goffs were left to their own devices. This forced the organization to stand back and look objectively at both its own situation and that of the general thoroughbred market. The outcome must have given rise to optimism and confidence because it resulted in large-scale plans being laid for the company's own sales ring.

Building started without delay, and as early as September 1975 the sale of yearlings was held in the new premises in County Kildare. At the same time the company's management was taken over by new people who brought a fresh initiative into it.

Apart from the privately owned Goff company, there is a non-profit-making auctioneering company in Ireland – the Ballsbridge International Bloodstock Sales, which feeds any profit it makes back into the Irish thoroughbred industry. This company has also intensified its efforts in recent years, having built a new sales centre at the RDS and appointed a new chairman.

The year 1866 saw another significant event, the running of the first Irish Derby. This was a further milestone in the history of the Irish thoroughbred industry, even though it was several years before this particular race gained significance as a test of breeding.

Towards the end of the nineteenth century, a small number of breeders, notably Mr Edward Kennedy, Col. William Hall-Walker and Major Eustace Loder, were successful in producing what, for the first time, was clearly recognizable as a relatively independent Irish breed. Kennedy, breeder of The Tetrarch and Dark Ronald, was later made President of Goff's Bloodstock Sales. Col. Hall-Walker founded the stud later to become the National Stud and was also responsible for introducing the Aga Khan to thoroughbred racing and breeding. Catnip, grand-dam of Nearco, was bred at the stud owned by Major Eustace Loder. He also owned the mare, Pretty Polly, who is to be found in the pedigree of Brigadier Gerard and Grundy, two of the most successful racehorses of our time.

Two of the present-day Irish studs, Gilltown and Sheshoon, were both founded shortly after the First World War. The latter belonged to the Aga Khan, who had just started to take an interest in thoroughbred racing and breeding. It was under the management of Sir Harry Greer, who was also director of the National Stud.

In most cases, a close relationship exists between a breeder and his horses in Ireland. A horse's environment also influences its character. A breeder of Connemara ponies often lives in a small cottage and keeps his horses in the land surrounding it (above left).
Hunters are more likely to be kept in the stables of large tradition-bound houses (Scarteen, Tipperary – above right).

Steeplechasers are usually housed in simple functional stables (below left) while the boxes for stallions in the National Stud are almost feudal in their magnificence (below right)

Ragusa Stud is a recent extension of Ardenode Stud, one of the leading studs in Ireland today. It is named after Ragusa (Ribof–Fantan II) perhaps the stud's best produce. Ardenode Stud is situated in Ballymore Eustace in Co. Kildare, the county most suitable for thoroughbred breeding. Ballymore, Flair Path and Guillaume Tell are currently at stud

Gilltown orginally belonged to Lord Furness, but at the time of the 'economic war' between Britain and Ireland he moved to the Gillingham Stud in Dorset – later to become the British National Stud. Gilltown then also passed into the hands of the Aga Khan, who by this time was very involved in thoroughbred breeding.

At about the same time the Irish National Stud was also beginning to make its name. Its history dates back to the turn of the century when the Scotsman William Hall-Walker bought some land and a few buildings in Tully, County Kildare, for the purpose of breeding thoroughbreds. In his first year he bred two winners and in subsequent years he built up a very influential stock. By 1914 he had produced seven winners of classic races. Col. Hall-Walker's successes are particularly interesting in that his methods of breeding were quite unique. His way of planning was looked upon as grotesque and eccentric, the reason for this being that he firmly believed in astrology. It is said that he matched mares and stallions according to their signs of the Zodiac, and that he made out a horoscope for each foal born. If its outlook was bad, he would sell the foal, irrespective of its appearance or any other qualities it might possess. So it happened that he sold Prince Palatine, who later won the St Leger and, on two occasions, the Ascot Gold Cup. Nevertheless, for eleven years he was one of the four most successful breeders in the British Isles. It is most likely that his success was not due to his belief in astrology, a quirk that has perhaps been given undue emphasis, but rather as a consequence of his extremely systematic methods.

We do know, however, that in 1907 the Colonel was one of the few to oppose the idea of exporting first-class stallions abroad, an opinion more indicative of practical foresight than astrological divination. He also proved himself a realist in that he energetically propounded the opinion that competition should also exist outside the racecourse.

He is perhaps best remembered for offering his stud to the British Government in 1915. Apart from its buildings and land, it comprised six stallions, forty-three brood mares, ten two-year-olds, nineteen yearlings and approximately three hundred head of cattle. After long negotiations the British Government accepted his generous offer, and thus Tully became the British National Stud. It produced first-class horses up to 1943: Blandford, Big Game and Sun Chariot were among its famous products.

In 1943, Tully passed into the hands of the Irish Government, and two years later the Irish National Stud Company was formed, specifically to protect Irish interests. Today Tully is a beautiful stud with accommodation for more than 200 horses, and with 836 acres of grazing land. Horses bred there have to date won fourteen classic races and approximately £800,000. Its present stallions include Tudor Music, Lord Gayle, Linacre, Giolla Mear, African Sky, Sallust, Tepukei, and Crash Course. They are available to Irish breeders on very easy terms. Other activities of the stud include the training of stud personnel, study into the best ways of keeping horses and managing studs, research into equestrian diseases, the maintenance of a library, and many more.

Thoroughbred breeding as a private enterprise developed in Ireland in the years after the war in much the same way as in other countries. The lines of the stallions Nearco, Hyperion and Fair Trial have dominated throughout, and their influence is evident even today. Breeding in Ireland was given a great advantage over other countries when in 1969 the Government granted the industry income tax concessions. This step was probably motivated by the amount of jobs which it was able to offer. In any case, it gave a great boost to the bloodstock industry. Massive capital investment on the part of foreign breeders followed, and a greater number of first-class stallions and mares than ever before were brought to Ireland. This, in turn, improved the situation for Irish breeders.

In the long run, the improved circumstances also gave opportunities for expansion to smaller breeders who became more important. Because they owned only one or two mares, they had to plan how to put them to the best use. For example, the breeder of Rheingold owned only two mares, and that of Giacometti, just its dam.

The economic crisis of 1974 affected thoroughbred breeding throughout the world. However, not all its side-effects were negative. The continuously rising standard of living before the crisis meant that, even in Ireland, animals of first-class quality were not the only ones to be used for breeding. Because of the growth of the racing industry everywhere, markets were readily available for horses of more inferior quality. One of the more positive outcomes of the crisis was that this particular trend ceased: while the best animals continued to hold their own, buyers could no longer be found for second-rate horses.

In Ireland breeders are counting on the thoroughbred market picking up again after the economic recession. Any misgivings which might be expressed – for example, that America might present a serious threat to the Irish market – are ignored, probably with justification. On the one hand, it will never be possible to export all racehorses to Europe, and on the other, only a very small percentage of American thoroughbreds are of the type suitable for European methods of racing.

Great hopes for the future are vested not only in Ireland's long-standing customers such as Australia, New Zealand and Japan, but more recently in South American countries and Iran, where there is a growing interest in racing. Whether or not this optimism is justified remains to be seen. The fact is, however, that at the present time the British racing industry – which has always been Ireland's best market – is suffering a serious crisis owing to taxation and organizational difficulties.

Steeplechasers

The steeplechaser is peculiar to breeding in Ireland and Britain. Half-bred and thoroughbred chasers are distinguished according to their ancestry, but their function is the same. Although the latter of the two clearly belongs among the thoroughbred types, they are bred in so specialized a fashion that they could almost be said to be a breed in their own right. This type of horse is little known on the Continent, but in Britain and Ireland it is used for National Hunt racing, the races for hunter-types so popular there.

The early steeplechases involved not only hunters, but also thoroughbreds with a special talent for jumping. However, as time passed, subsequent breeding, which was always directed towards a specified goal, produced pure thoroughbreds and, from the hunters, half-bred chasers. Common breeding objectives ultimately resulted in a common type of horse with different ancestry. By the end of the nineteenth century it is likely that half-bred chasers were already being specially produced: an observer remarked around that time that 'cocktails' (offspring of a thoroughbred stallion and a light, half-bred mare), a common sight on the racecourse a quarter of a century earlier, would not now stand a chance.

It must be pointed out that the greatest number of chasers are bred specially for a particular task. Only in very exceptional cases are Irish steeplechasers 'converted' and re-trained as flat-racers. There are recognized 'jumper' families, whose progeny are very likely to have jumping talent. On the other hand the descendants of these very 'jumper' families, have also often turned out to be horses with above-average talent for flat-racing.

In relation to these 'jumper' families, a strange fact about chaser breeding is worth mentioning: top-class chasers have often been sired by stallions who have never jumped in their lives. This fact has often been used by some writers – albeit the rather short-sighted ones – to argue that a talent for jumping is not hereditary. This is not so. It is true that these stallions have never jumped, but this does not necessarily mean that they possess no latent jumping potential. Stallions at stud often have never had the opportunity to show any potential talents they might possess. If they have shown above-average ability on the flat, they are sent to stud after four or five years, without ever having been ridden over a fence.

It usually takes ten to twelve years for a steeplechaser to be sufficiently mature to carry heavy weights over long distances and difficult jumps. A stallion is seldom suitable for activities such as these, which require a good deal of composure. Most successful chasers are therefore geldings, and a small number, mares. The Irish judge a stallion's ability to breed useful chasers by the jumping ability of its relations or of progeny it has already sired.

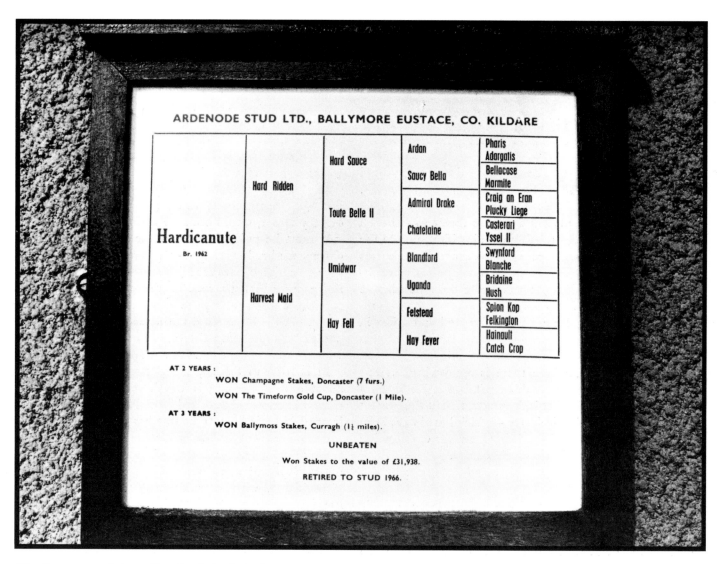

ARDENODE STUD LTD., BALLYMORE EUSTACE, CO. KILDARE

			Ardan	Pharis / Adargatis
Hardicanute Br. 1962	Hard Ridden	Hard Sauce		
			Saucy Bella	Bellacose / Marmite
		Toute Belle II	Admiral Drake	Craig an Eran / Plucky Liege
			Chatelaine	Casterari / Yssel II
	Harvest Maid	Umidwar	Blandford	Swynford / Blanche
			Uganda	Bridaine / Hush
		Hay Fell	Felstead	Spion Kop / Felkington
			Hay Fever	Hainault / Catch Crop

AT 2 YEARS :
    WON Champagne Stakes, Doncaster (7 furs.)
    WON The Timeform Gold Cup, Doncaster (1 Mile).

AT 3 YEARS :
    WON Ballymoss Stakes, Curragh (1½ miles).

UNBEATEN

Won Stakes to the value of £31,938.

RETIRED TO STUD 1966.

Hardicanute, one of the stallions in Ardenode Stud, came as a yearling into the possession of P. J. Prendergast, one of the best trainers in Ireland and in the world. Whilst still with Prendergast, he ran twice as a two-year-old and won both races. These successes led him to be looked on as favourite for the English Derby in the following year. This, however, was not to come about as he only ran once more as a three-year-old

Nevertheless he later won this race, after which he was returned to stud at Ardenode, having won stakes totalling £31,938. Since 1966 his progeny have won more than 125 races and more than £300,000.
His most famous progeny is his son Hard to Beat who won the 1972 French Derby and came third in the Prix de l' Arc de Triomphe. In 1972 Hardicanute was voted the best stallion in Europe

Lord Gayle (Sir Gaylord–Sticky Case) was bred in the USA. Altogether he won eight races, in the United States, France and England. At the moment he belongs to the National Stud

Tudor Music (Tudor Melody–Fran) is another National Stud stallion. He is the colt of an excellent stallion whose progeny between them have won stakes of over £800,000

Whistling Wind (Whistler–Good as Gold) also belonged at one time to the National Stud. He only ran as a two-year-old, when he won two races in Ireland and England. He is now in Japan

St Alphage (Red God–Sallydeans), like most stallions, is owned by a syndicate. He has won ten races over distances ranging from 1000 to 1200 metres, proving himself thereby to be an excellent sprinter

Will Somers (Tudor Minstrel–Queen's Jest) has never been a particularly successful racer, but has nevertheless turned out to be successful in breeding. Among others, he has sired a number of good steeplechasers

Bold Lad (Bold Ruler–Barn Pride) should not be confused with the American horse of the same name. He stands in Kildangan Stud in Co. Kildare, one of the largest studs in Ireland

Pall Mall (Palestine–Malapert) was bred by the Queen. He is a classic racer and has won the English 2000 guineas. He has also been extremely successful in breeding

Karabas (Worden II–Fair Share) showed promise when still a foal and was sold for £2000. He lived up to his reputation and later won over $200,000 in many countries

The choice of a stallion is also influenced by a further consideration: £850,553 was spent on the 882 National Hunt races held in 1976, a smaller sum than that spent on the smaller number of flat races. This indicates that it is likely that, on average, less money will be made on a steeplechaser than on a flat racehorse. In order to make National Hunt racing economically worthwhile, the breeding of a chaser has to be a less expensive process than that of a flat racehorse. For this reason, first-class stallions, whose stud fees would run into thousands, are not used for siring chasers; instead breeders select stallions whose appearance or ancestry is reasonably good but whose talent for racing is perhaps no better than average. Stayer types are an obvious preference. Arkle's sire was one such stallion. He had a classic pedigree but no particular talent for racing. Another sire of first-class chasers, Vulgan, had incredible staying power, but never ran in a steeplechase in his life.

For this reason, the Irish pay particular attention to the dam's side when breeding steeplechasers. It is considered obligatory that she comes from a 'jumper' family. She supplies the basis of the line in that she plays a greater part in chaser breeding than the stallion. Of all the thoroughbred mares in Britain and Ireland, one-fifth are used for the breeding of steeplechasers; nearly 60 per cent of these are in Ireland.

The development of steeplechaser-breeding more or less parallels that of thoroughbred-breeding; both experienced the same periods of progress and depression. Then it began to look as though the market, limited as it was to England and Ireland, no longer needed as many steeplechasers. The demand for flat-racers increased to such an extent that higher prices were being paid for inferior flat-racers than for first-class chasers. Flat-racers were being sold as foals or yearlings in order to bring quicker financial returns. Potential steeplechasers, on the other hand, are normally kept until they are three or four years old. Owing to the resulting lessening of the demand for chasers, many steeplechase trainers were forced to meet the demands of the market with flat-racers of inferior quality.

Since only a small number of these horses could cope with the demands put on them, the value of genuine chasers rose sharply. Their market became more stable as the thoroughbred market suffered the 1974 crisis. In fact, the market for steeplechasers is managing to remain stable and will survive the present recession in British racing. The fact that young horses are kept at home for three to four years is of advantage to the steeplechaser-breeding industry: a foal destined to be a flat-racer, which is born in a year of economic crisis, means an almost certain loss for its breeder, whereas the breeder of a chaser can reckon with the financial situation having stabilized by the time his horse is ready for selling, two or three years later.

Irish Draught and Hunter Breeding

The hunter is not a breed in itself, but a cross between a thoroughbred and an Irish Draught. In earlier times the breeding of Irish Draught horses was a separate branch of Irish horse-breeding, having as its main objective the production of work horses. Nowadays, however, the Irish Draught is pure-bred only because it is necessary in the breeding of hunters.

The history of the Irish Draught begins around the sixteenth century. Its ancestors were the Hobbies, the horses of medieval Ireland. These, in turn, were products of the crossing of imported Spanish and Oriental horses with native Celtic ponies. Most Irish breeds, in fact are descended from these Hobbies. They are also the ancestors of those Irish horses which, together with later Oriental imports, founded the thoroughbred stock. The fact that Irish Draughts, thoroughbreds and Connemara ponies all have the same origins is a probable explanation for the excellent progeny which crossing one breed with the other seems to have brought about.

In the eighteenth century, the later distinct divisions of horse-breeding were already becoming evident. Horses were being bred specifically for racing and specifically for work. As agriculture developed, more intensive farming methods required a heavier type of horse. Most farmers, however, were poor and could not afford to import draught horses. They compromised by singling out the heaviest horses from the animals at their disposal, and, because horses were only imported in exceptional cases, the horses used retained their quality as good horses to ride. It is also likely that the farmers kept this particular quality in mind when breeding them: they felt it desirable to own a horse suitable for a variety of tasks.

In the mid-nineteenth century the breeding of Irish Draughts was granted a subsidy by the state, as it had got into difficult straits during the Great Famine between 1845 and 1850. Fortunately, conditions improved shortly after that, and a small number of draught horses were even exported. One such horse, the stallion Nabocklish, rose to fame; his son Schlutter was founder of a line of Hanoverian stallions.

At the beginning of the present century some people must have had the notion of 'improving' the breed by crossing it with Clydesdale and Suffolk – both famous draught breeds. Luckily their efforts did not come to much because of the government's decision in 1917 to authorize the registration of Irish Draughts and to commission an inspection into their breeding. This move was an attempt to put the breeding of half-bred horses under state control. Of the 1450 horses presented, only 375 mares and forty-four stallions were registered. Preference was given to horses of a true-bred type. This inspection took place at a bad time, however, as the number of horses was small and unrepresentative, owing to the large numbers exported to countries involved in the war.

After that, inspections were carried out annually. The The Irish Draught section of Bórd na gCapall's Irish Horse Register now contains around 1100 mares and 70 stallions. The influence of Clydesdales and Shires on the breed became increasingly weaker, and since 1968 no more have been entered.

The situation of Irish Draught breeding today is roughly as follows: only very seldom are horses bred for working; by far the greatest number are used for the breeding of hunters. However, in order that the Irish Draught should continue to exist as a breed in its own right, not all the mares are covered by thoroughbred stallions.

Although the breeding costs are the same, a much higher price can be obtained for a hunter. To overcome this problem, which is, after all, in the long run threatening the future of hunter-breeding, the state has had to step in. In retrospect, it can be said that this help came at the right time. Fortunately it happened that, in relation to the negotiations for Ireland's entry into the EEC, a survey was made on the circumstances of the Irish agricultural and horse-breeding industries. In 1965 a team was set up by the government to carry out the survey with the brief to make recommendations for any improvements it saw necessary. In this way every aspect of breeding and equestrian sport – apart from the thoroughbred industry – was examined in detail.

The most significant outcome of this inquiry seems to have been the setting up of a central authority to look after the interests of the true-bred horse industry. This authority, recommended by the investigating team still exists today, under the name of the Irish Horse Board, or in Irish, Bórd na gCapall. Its function as regards the breeding of Irish Draughts and hunters is the payment of grants and subsidies.

Nowadays Irish Draught breeding is subsidized in the form of rearing grants paid for each foal born. Owners of certain chosen mares are further subsidized by being reimbursed for stud fees paid for servicing by recommended stallions. The size of this grant is planned in such a way as to make ownership of a Draught mare a viable economic proposition, even if the animal is still being used for farm-work. This improvement has meant that Draught breeding is no longer under threat. If the politics involved in its breeding continue to be as adaptable to changing circumstances, then there is no reason for anyone to worry.

The ideal horse for hunting can be produced from the Irish Draught with its robustness and calmness, refined by mixing it with thoroughbred qualities such as speed and endurance. Neither breed really possesses characteristics which would be disadvantageous for a hunter. It is

well known that the result of this so-called practical cross-breeding turned out to be the very best. One good reason for this was that the thoroughbred and Irish Draught had been consolidated breeds for a long time. Furthermore, both had common ancestors in the Hobbies. The occasional 'refreshing' which the Irish Draught breed acquired through the few attempts to mix some thoroughbred blood into it, must have also been for the best. All in all, hunter-breeding must be looked upon as a crossing of two related breeds, a crossing which has shown and which still shows a high level of understanding and subtlety on the part of the breeders.

To a certain extent it was necessity which brought about this successful cross-breeding. Being an island, Ireland is somewhat isolated, and it seemed best to use the horses already there to produce the type of horse wanted. But in addition to this, the Irish are shrewd enough to know how to tackle the job, and they also possess all the expertise in equine matters needed to experiment with cross-breeding. Without much effort they can breed heavier, more elegant or smaller horses at will, with the help of two different breeds. If a breeder has his Draught mare served by a thoroughbred stallion, he is likely to produce a heavy hunter. If he wanted a middle- or lightweight hunter, he would simply cross the progeny of a Draught/thoroughbred mating with a thoroughbred stallion which, for its own part, could be lighter or heavier as required. If he were to mix some pony blood into his breed, he would produce smaller hunters. There are no limits to the breeding experiments he could carry out.

Since the middle of the last century the breeding of hunters has been closely associated with the history of the Royal Dublin Society. The RDS had been founded about a hundred years earlier by a small group of Irishmen who felt that governmental efforts to develop Ireland's agriculture and trade needed supplementing. To encourage horse-breeding, then an important branch of agriculture, they began to organize shows around 1850. Only later did the government subsidize their efforts, and even then its main contribution up to 1934 merely consisted of the registration of hunter and Draught mares. and thoroughbred stallions. Then things changed. In 1934

Left: Except in a few cases, it is normally impossible for the act of copulation to be carried out naturally in thoroughbred breeding – the risks of injury to the stallion are too high. To protect the stallion, the mare is usually held down forcibly

 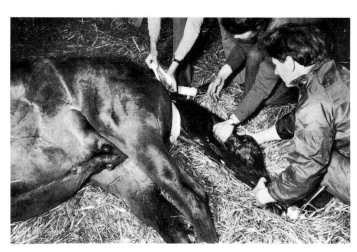

Although horses are generally born without much difficulty, a thoroughbred mare is carefully watched when giving birth. She is usually put into a special labour stable which is connected to a

 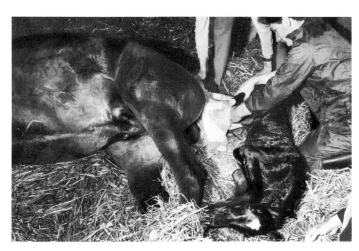

waiting room by a small window. This affords the least disturbance to the mare. The watchers only intervene when the mare gets ready for the birth. The actual birth, for which most mares lie down,

 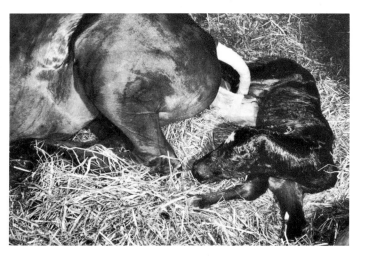

starts with the breaking of the waters and the appearance of the sac. This mare is Lady Symons, privately owned, but who was brought to the National Stud to give birth

116

a strict set of laws was passed regulating all aspects of the breeding of half-bred horses, and thus bringing the breeding of hunters under state control. For example, any stallion over two years old, whose owner was not intending to geld him, had now to be certified annually. These certificates were only awarded when the stallion in question could meet a number of exacting requirements with regard to its health, performance and appearance. Thoroughbred stallions which were to be used for the breeding of half-bred horses also came under this legislation. Apart from the usual defects and shortcomings, no animal suffering from scales, laminitis, spavin, etc, was allowed to pass. In this way they underwent more exacting tests than are usual in horse-breeding. These conditions are still in operation today and, to a large extent, account for the high quality of Irish horses. At the moment approximately 500 stallions are licensed in this way, three-quarters of which are thoroughbreds and the rest Irish Draughts and half-breds. Only since 1972 have half-bred stallions, once again, been allowed to be used for stud – they had been banned from it for a few years before that. It was generally believed that only thoroughbreds were capable of passing on to the next generation a sufficient share of the qualities of hardiness and endurance.

Most of the thoroughbred stallions used for hunter breeding in the country today belong to the government. As they are relatively expensive to buy, the government usually undertakes their purchase and rents them out to interested stud-farmers. In this way, stallions can be used for special breeding purposes, and exchanged whenever required. Owners of mares receive subsidies in the form of allowances for foals and compensation for stud-fees, provided the mare can meet certain requirements, and has been served by a registered stallion. Up to now, compensation has been paid out to approximately 8000 mare owners. About half of these have foals eligible for grants.

Each of these functions is now the responsibility of Bórd na gCapall.

Right: Not only climate and geographical surroundings influence the development of a young horse. It is equally important that a foal has a general feeling of well being. Often it will express this feeling in, among other things, its desire to move about. A breeder, in fact, can judge a foal's state of health by watching how much it moves about

The character of a growing horse is most likely to develop positively when an intimate and undisturbed relationship exists between foal and dam. For this reason, even-tempered horses make the best brood mares. If a mare, successful in her sporting career, is to be used for breeding, she must be carefully prepared for her new role

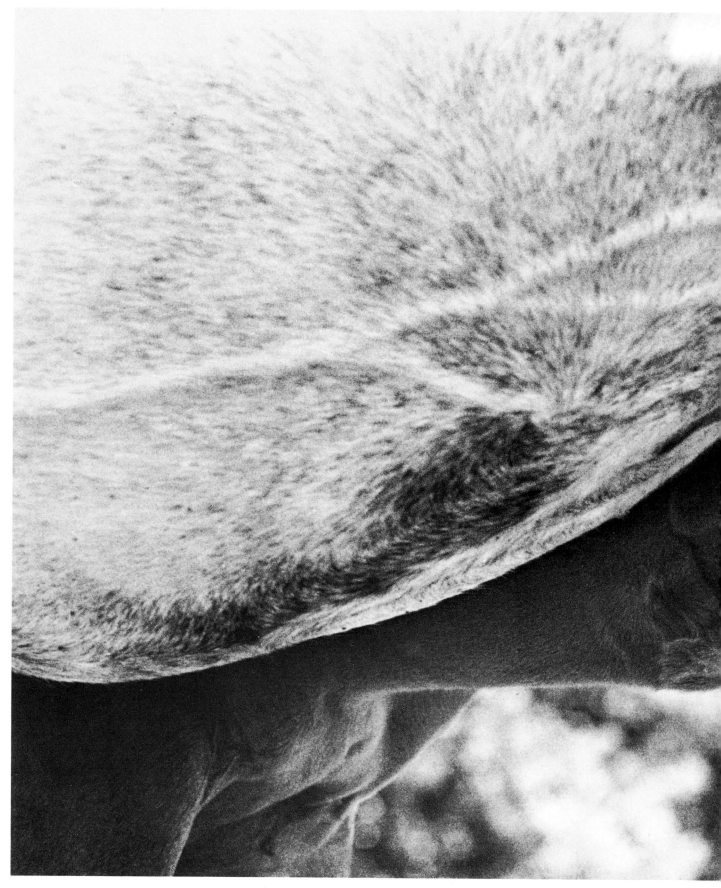

A foal's desire to suckle can be an indication of its health and contentedness just as much as its drive to move about

The contentedness of most foals in Ireland comes from the fact that they can grow up among their own kind and are always treated as horses

Ponies

Ponies play a more important part in equestrian sport in Ireland and Britain than anywhere else in the world, and they are therefore bred on a relatively large scale.

The centre for Irish pony-breeding has always been Connemara, the home of the original Irish ponies. Unfortunately, much of the history of the Connemara pony is based on speculation, most of which seems quite incredible. The actual origin of the breed, however, is clearer. It dates back to prehistoric times, when the Celts came to Ireland. In the years that followed, the Celts continued to breed the small horses which they had brought with them, without any significant outside influence. In the Middle Ages, rich Galway merchants who traded with Spain crossed Spanish and Andalusian horses with the native breed.

More concrete evidence of the breeding of Connemara ponies exists from the mid-nineteenth century, when Arab and thoroughbred blood was crossed with the breed, and, towards the end of the century, Welsh pony stallions were also imported, whose progeny seems to have been generally satisfactory.

Around the turn of the century, the government commissioned an examination into the breeding of Connemara ponies. Professor Ewart from Edinburgh was appointed to look into the existing circumstances, and, if necessary, to suggest areas of improvement. The recommendations made by the professor could briefly be summed up as follows: the state should subsidize the breed by purchasing the best stallions, material for a stud book should be gathered, and an order should be issued that only chosen, recommended stallions be used for stud.

It was not until 1923 that a breeding association was formed and most of Ewart's recommendations put into operation. Three years later the first stud book was published. From a large number of ponies, only seventy-five mares and six stallions were chosen and entered. From then on the breeding of ponies has been under strict control, and it has been carried out with great foresight and competence. Government subsidies continued to be large, and the association was able to buy its own stallions and place them in centres throughout Connemara. An annual show held in Clifden provides a means of keeping a regular check on the breed.

In 1966 an examination of the situation by the government showed surprisingly good results, which nevertheless still left some room for improvement. In the meantime, the stud book had been closed (i.e., only horses both of whose parents were already entered could be added to it). Now it contains around 3000 mares, 200 stallions and 125 geldings. The only area where some improvement is still called for is that of the training of young ponies. Many breeders lack either the skill to train young horses or the facilities to do so. Ponies which are sold unschooled fetch a smaller price than those which are trained, especially if they are intended as mounts for children.

Connemara pony breeding will survive without any great difficulty, for the simple reason that the quality of these small horses is incomparable.

Irish Horseman-
ship

A horse fair

As we neared the town of Drumcurran the fact that we were on our way to a horse fair became alarmingly apparent. It is impossible to imagine how we pursued an uninjured course through the companies of horsemen, the crowded carts, the squealing colts, the irresponsible led horses, and, most immutable of all obstacles, the groups of country-women, with the hoods of their heavy blue cloaks over their heads . . .

It was eleven o'clock, and the fair was in full swing. Its vortex was in the centre of the field below us, where a low bank of sods and earth had been erected as a trial jump, with a yelling crowd of men and boys at either end, acting instead of the usual wings to prevent a swerve. Strings of reluctant horses were scourged over the bank by dozens of willing hands, while exhortation, cheers, and criticism were freely showered upon each performance.

'Give the knees to the saddle, boy, and leave the heels slack.' 'That's a nice horse. He'd keep a jock on his back where another'd throw him!' 'Well jumped, begor! She fled that fairly!' as an ungainly three-year-old flounced over the bank without putting a hoof on it. Then her owner, unloosing his pride in simile after the manner of his race:

'Ah ha! when she give a lep, man, she's that free, she's like a hare for it!'*

* From Somerville and Ross, see Note, p. 187.

The concept 'Irish horsemanship' is extremely difficult to explain.

There is no problem when you are sitting among friends talking about it, when you are able to listen quietly and understand exactly what someone is saying, when the gaps in your own experiences are filled in by the stories and anecdotes of others who know much more about the subject than you do, when the ice-cubes in your whisky (or, more accurately, whiskey) tinkle briskly and a fire glows in the fire-place.

The problems start when you try to re-tell – particularly in writing – what was talked about.

Perhaps this can best be done in a roundabout fashion. After all, the background to 'that special relationship between man and horse which makes Ireland a land of horses through and through' is the relationship itself.

Let us start with an un-Irish name, from the circus – an almost sacrilegiously different world: Fredy Knie, Senior.

In the preface to Klaus Zeeb's behavioural study *Horses trained by Fredy Knie*, Fredy Knie himself tells of how, at a particular stage in his many years of training, he learnt a lesson which was to have a profound effect on his relationship with horses:

And then I had a third teacher, a man who had only started to work with horses relatively late in life. He had little time for theory and relied to a large extent on instinct and feelings. He usually managed to get a horse to do what he wanted it to do by showing affection and sympathy. This third teacher was someone upon whom I later came to model myself. He taught me that it was always *my* fault when Rablo, the horse I was training at the time, made mistakes, in that I had not sufficiently responded to the horse. After that I was able to go to lunch after training sessions with a greater feeling of achievement and satisfaction than before. Herr Schmidt, as my third teacher was called (he originally came from Budapest), showed me that horses were not stupid or stubborn; stubbornness is much more likely to be a human quality, or so I think at least. I now always blame myself for any mistake, not the horse. In this way I gradually built up my own theory and,

in a manner of speaking, my own education. One of the ways I kept a check on my activities was to work with an open door. I had discovered how valuable it was to let the public watch when I was trying things out, for, if the public is present during training sessions and trials, you have to be totally in control of what is happening. This turned out to be of great advantage to me. I learnt to be my own judge and teacher, and in doing so began to study the nature of my horses. I came to know their personalities and discovered many emotions which I recognized from humans – love, jealousy, indeed anything you might care to name – for it seems that such emotions are as common to horses as to human beings.

I hope I can be excused for making what might look like a somewhat sudden and obscure connection at this point: what Fredy Knie, Senior, had to work out painstakingly is something that comes naturally to the Irish.

Under totally different circumstances and, to some extent, by other methods, he built up a relationship between a man and a horse whose impulse would normally be generated by landscape, tradition, custom and – last but not least – a sense of business.

Irish horsemanship has always been a source of inspiration for writers. Michael McLaverty's story *The Old White Mare* was never intended as a piece of literary showmanship. It is a story, simply conceived and simply written, about an old man's love for his horse. It is a good example of the close association which exists in Ireland between, on the one hand, the sort of cunning sense of business mentioned already, and, on the other, the people's affection for their horses. It could also be said that the story shows that these two qualities are, nevertheless, very different. Only in Ireland can contrasts such as these be found:

Paddy crossed to the stable and the mare nickered when she heard his foot on the cobbled street. Warm hay-scented air met him as he opened the door. Against the wall stood the white mare. She cocked her ears and turned her head towards the light. She was big and fat with veins criss-crossing on her legs like dead ivy roots on the limbs of a tree. Her eyes were wet-shining and black, their upper lids fringed with long grey lashes. Paddy stroked her neck and ran his fingers through her yellow-grey mane.

A collar with the straw sticking out of it was soon buckled on, and with chains rattling from her sides he led her through

Previous page: unposed family portrait. Three generations of hunters

the stone-slap into the field. He looked at the sky, at the sea with its patches of mist, and then smilingly went to his plough. Last evening the coulter was cutting too deep and he now adjusted it, giving it a final smack with the spanner that rang out clear in the morning air. The mare was sniffing the rain-wet grass under the hedge and she raised her head jerkily as he approached, sending a shower of cold drops from the bushes down his neck. He shivered but spoke kindly to the beast as he led her to be tackled. In a few minutes all was ready, and gripping the handles in God's name, he ordered the horse forward, and his day's work began.

The two sisters eyed him from the window. His back was towards them. Above the small stone fence they could see his bent figure, his navy-blue trousers with a brown patch on the seat of them, his grey shirt sleeves, the tattered back of his waistcoat, and above his shabby hat the swaying quarters of the mare.

'Did you ever see such a man since God made you! I declare to goodness he'll kill that mare,' said Martha;

'It's himself he'll kill if he's not careful. Let me bold Paddy be laid up after this and 'tis the last field he'll plough, for I'll sell the mare, done beast and all as she is!' replied Kate, pressing her face closer to the window ...

But in the morning he didn't get up. His shoulders, arms and legs were stiff and painful. Martha brought him his breakfast, and it was a very subdued man that she saw.

'Give me a lift up, Martha, on the pillows. That's a good girl. Aisy now, aisy!' he said in a slow, pained voice.

'Do you feel bad, Paddy?'

'Bravely, Martha, bravely. There's a wee pain across me shoulder, maybe you'd give it a rub. I'll be all right now when I get a rest.'

'You took too much out of yourself for one day.'

'I know, I know! But it'd take any other man three days to do the same field. Listen, Martha, put the mare out on the side of the hill; a canter round will do her a world of good.'

And so the first day wore on with his limbs aching, Martha coming to attend him, or Kate coming to counsel him. But from his bed he could see the mare clear as a white rock on the face of the hill, and it heartened him to watch her long tail busily swishing. On the bed beside him was his stick and on the floor a battered biscuit tin. Hour after hour he struck the tin with his stick when he wanted something – matches, tobacco, a drink or his shoulder rubbed. And glad he was if Martha answered his knocking.

Two days passed in this way, and on the morning of the third the boat with the dealer was due. Time and again Martha went out on a hill at the back of the house, scanning the sea for the boat. At last she saw it and hurried to Kate with the news. Kate made a big bowl of warm punch and brought it to Paddy.

'How do you feel this morning?' she said when she entered the room.

'A lot aisier, thank God, a lot aisier.'

'Take this now and turn in and sleep. It'll do you good.'

Paddy took the warm bowl in his two hands, sipping slowly, and giving an odd cough as the strong whisky caught his breath. Whenever he paused his eyes were on the window watching the mare on the hillside, and when he had finished, he sighed and lay back happily. His body felt deliciously warm and he smiled sweetly. Poor Kate; he misjudged her; she has a heart of corn and means well. Warm eddies of air flowed slowly through his head, stealing into every corner, filling him with a thoughtless ecstasy, and closing his eyes in sleep.

As he slept the dealer came, and the mare was sold. When he wakened he felt a queer emptiness in the room as if something had been taken from it. Instinctively he turned to the window and looked out. The mare was nowhere to be seen and the stone-slap had been tumbled. He seized his stick and battered impatiently on the biscuit tin. He was about to get out of bed when Kate came into the room.

'The mare has got out of the field!'

'She has that and what's more she'll never set foot in it again.'

He waited, waited to hear the worst, that she was sick or had a broken a leg.

'The dealer was here an hour ago and I sold her, and, let me tell you, I got a good penny for her,' she added a little proudly.

His anger sent a quickening flame through him, and he looked at his sister, his eyes fiercely bright and his mouth open. Catching the rail of the bed he raised himself into a sitting posture and glared at her.

'Lie down, Paddy, like a good man and quieten yourself. Sure we did it for your own good,' she said, trying to make light of it, and fixing the clothes up around his chest. 'What was she but a poor bit of a beast dying with age. And a good bargain we made.'

'Bargain, is it? And me after rearing her since she was a wee foal. No; he'll not get her, I tell you! He'll not get her!'

'For the love of God, man, have sense, have reason!'

But he wasn't listening, he threw back the clothes and reached for his trousers. He brushed her aside with his arm, and his hands trembled as he put on his boots. He seized his stick and made for the door. They tried to stop him and he raised his stick to them. 'Don't meddle with me or I'll give you a belt with this!'

He was out, taking the short-cut down by the back of the

Ireland's green is mixed with the dark blue of the lakes, the yellow of gorse, the red of fuchsia. Even in the smallest towns and villages, houses with brightly painted façades are to be seen. Nestling close together, they crouch along the roadside, belying the disturbing contrasts they often conceal. Bright colours against monotony – often the brightly coloured exterior is a front which distracts from the poverty which exists behind it

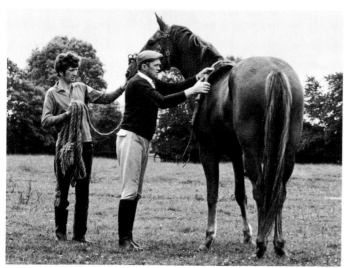

Some Irish trainers specialize in familiarizing three- and four-year-olds with their future careers in show-jumping. One such trainer is Willie Ryan in Co. Tipperary. He either takes in the horses of his breeder friends or buys unbroken horses and sells them again when they are broken in. Unfortunately many breeders lack the means and skill to train their horses themselves. On the whole, dealers and buyers prefer to buy not the raw, unbroken animals, but those which can already demonstrate their capabilities. Significantly higher prices are paid for these horses

house, across the hills that led to the quay. He might be in time; they'd hardly have her in the boat yet. Stones in the gaps fell with a crash behind him and he didn't stop to build them up, not caring where sheep strayed or cattle either. His eyes were fixed on the sea, on the mainland where Maggie was going. His heart hammered wildly, hammered with sharp stinging pains, and he had to halt to ease himself.

He thought of his beast, the poor beast that hated noise and fuss, standing nervous on the pier with a rope tied round her four legs. Gradually the rope would tighten and she would topple with a thud on the uneven stones while the boys around would cheer. It was always a sight for the young, this shipping of beasts in the little sailing boats. The thought maddened him. His breath wheezed and he licked his dry salt lips.

And soon he came on to the road that swept in a half circle to the quay. He saw the boat and an oar sticking over the side. He wouldn't have time to go round. Below him jutted a neck of rock near which the boat would pass on her journey out. He might be able to hail them.

He splashed his way through shallow sea-pools on to the rock, scrambled over its mane of wet seaweed, until he reached the farthest point. Sweat was streaming below his hat and he trembled weakly as he saw the black nose of the boat coming towards him. He saw the curling froth below her bow, the bending backs of the men, and heard the wooden thump of the oars. Nearer it came, gathering speed. A large wave tilted the boat and he saw the white side of his mare, lying motionless between the beams. They were opposite him now, a hundred yards from him. He raised his stick and called, but he seemed to have lost his voice. He waved and called again, his voice sounding strange and weak. The man in the stern waved back as he would to a child. The boat passed the rock, leaving a wedge of calm water in her wake. The noise of the oars stopped and the sail filled in the breeze. For a long time he looked at the receding boat, his spirit draining from him. A wave washed up the rock, frothing at his feet, and he turned wearily away, going slowly back the road that led home.

Take a horse-market anywhere in Ireland. A few houses clustered together. Few maps note their existence – who would want to know about them, anyway? It is hardly more of an occasion than a get-together of a few small farmers from the locality. Perhaps a few dealers from 'beyond' might have lost their way and ended up there. No top-quality animals will be shown and nobody bothers much about presentation.

No top-quality animals? Those in the know would

Right: McKee Barracks in Dublin is the training centre for the jumping team. On the training ground, a young rider demonstrates the ideas upon which his training has been based. As well as their knowledge of classic show-jumping methods, instructors here use their own experience and intuition when training. Irish show-jumpers and hunters are, above all, independent and are at their best when given a free head. Their balance is best and they are most observant and at ease when at half-rein

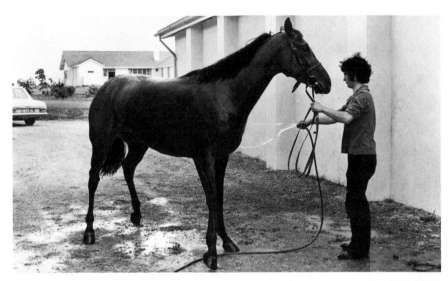

Phonsie O'Brien trains more than twenty horses in Golden, Tipperary. He has specialized in the training of steeplechasers. The atmosphere in most National Hunt stables is suited to this hardy sport; they are often noticeably different from the more smoothly run flat-racing stables

disagree. It is not always just the pedigree family trees which touch the clouds in Ireland. Nobody asks about a horse's ancestry when he likes what is being led clumsily on a rope before him.

Treasures turn up even in the smallest of places. Notice the subtle difference between 'treasures' and 'top-quality animals'. Worlds might separate them – if you were to use marketing criteria – but the small world which exists among that cluster of houses obliterates such boundaries.

Indeed, great horses are often born in this small world. Take, for example, Flanagan, ridden to fame by Pat Smythe, favourite of jumping enclosures all over the world, surrounded by an atmosphere of grandeur. In her book *Flanagan, My Friend* Pat Smythe writes:

Mothers have an important part to play in forming the character of their children, and Flanagan was no exception. His mother was a bay Irish Draught mare, big, plain and rather common, but a great character and an honest worker on the farm. She was typical of the basic type of mare that breeds the real Irish hunter. Sadly this wonderful foundation for breeding animals of substance and quality is gradually becoming more rare. Many young ones of this type suffered from the high prices paid by foreign butchers.

Flanagan's mother first 'kicked over the traces' after her day's work was done. It was evening time and she was grazing near a bank. She thought she heard the leprechauns and looked up, but there was no leprechaun; better by far, a young chestnut stallion was looking down on her from the bank. No one would have noticed the hair around his heels as he lightly leapt down to her side. Their love was blessed and less than a year later the mare had her own chestnut colt running by her side.

The farm where they lived was only a smallholding of grass, bog and drains, crumbling banks, broken gates and a bedstead end to block one big gap in a bank. Railways and tarmacked roads did not disturb their life. Even the old byre in the small yard was too low for the horses. This background gave the colt a happy childhood while he developed into a Wexford hunter type with good substance, standing on short legs. He benefited from the limestone land that he grazed through the warm days and nights, with the grass saturated in dew, a combination of factors that makes the Irish horse what he is.

Right: Polo – the oldest ball game in the world, played 2000 years ago by the Medes and Persians – is still played in Ireland. However, it is not very widespread and is looked on as separate from the other traditional equestrian sports

We must now return to that curious phenomenon, 'Irish time'. An Irishman has time for his horse – time, patience and nerves. If his horse is lame, he does not take it to the vet. He relies on the old dictum 'Put them on the grass!' Time heals all wounds.

A farmer or breeder may be heading for a definite goal, but, although he keeps this goal in mind, he does not rush at it. He knows about all the stages that are important in a horse's development. He also knows that the intervals between each stage are important too. The demands which he makes on his horse must grow naturally. In other words, the Irish have a horror of turning their horses into child prodigies.

In Ireland a horse can feel the sympathy of the people around it when it is being trained to perform those activities which, from the point of view of ability, it is well able to perform, but for which it nevertheless needs all the helpful encouragement it can get to master.

This training is not based on clever, sophisticated theories. It is both inseparable from and determined by natural experience, instinct, and the ability of the Irish to get the best out of a horse.

Let us go back to Pat Smythe's story of how Flanagan was trained:

Although the new chestnut had a plain face, it was full of character, from the tips of his long ears, and following the white star and stripe that runs in a crooked line down his nose, to the pendulous lower lip. His clown-like appearance earned him the name of 'Bud Flanagan', and not as an insult to the great artist of that name, the chestnut has been known as 'Flanagan' ever since.

The freedom of the Irish days was gone and 'the Brig' started to work on his green but unspoilt material. The horse could not have been in better hands for his breaking and early training. The experience of the trainer had been gained from a lifetime with horses, first graduating at the equitation school at Weedon in 1923, and then spending many years as an instructor of riding in the army. He had participated in many branches of the sport of riding, having won point-to-point races and show jumping events. He played polo, a great team game, and concentrated on schooling young horses, jumpers and polo ponies. Hunting played an important part too and he was Master of 'the Woolwich Drag' for four seasons.

Flanagan could not have fallen into better hands. Naturally, as his rider was an all rounder, he trained his horses to have the same versatility. So began the round of discipline with understanding that builds confidence and efficiency in the making of the young horse. Flanagan was subjected to a surcingle around his stomach, sometimes loose and at other times tight. He had to get used to mouthing bits that made him play with the mouthpiece and often slobber with the saliva caused by twiddling the little keys on the bit with his tongue. As the lessons progressed there were the bridle, the long reins, the lunging reins, the side reins, the saddle, the crupper and the lot.

The horse was never given a fright and having a natural capacity for enjoyment, he loved the rides over the open country with wide horizons and the fresh air. The sea was not far away and could be seen from some places, but it was the surrounding sights that kept most of the horse's attention. Most important were the other horses in the yard. There was always bustle and activity with cars coming and going and cats making their home in the hay rack, in the stables, the corner of the box or even the horse's back, as it suited the individual cat.

Lessons continued at his happy home and the horse was backed and began to learn to jump small places, which was no trouble to him after his youthful escapades solo over the Wexford banks. One day he had a bit of extra fun when being exercised early in the morning. He was about a quarter of a mile from home when he gave a buck and dropped his shoulder. Finding himself free, he galloped away along a green lane to the top of a high hill from where he could see miles of ocean. Tickled by the inspiring view, he galloped another mile and a half nearly to the railway station.

In his *Riding Recollections* (London, 1878) George John Whyte-Melville included a chapter on Irish hunters. Born the grandson of a duke in England, he was, appropriately, educated at Eton, after which he joined the army and became an officer in the Coldstream Guards. He grew up with horses and died with them when, on 5 December 1878, he fell from his horse in a hunting accident.

Time may have proved some of this writer's opinions wrong, but his knowledge and understanding of the most fundamental characteristics of hunting in Ireland – and thereby also of Irish horsemanship – remain relevant:

Where people live with horses, as they do in Ireland, their children are reared with horses. Relating to animals is taught as part of everyday living right from the start

In families which own horses, young children are often more steady on horseback than they are on their feet

Young boys and girls who confidently and cheerfully jump their ponies are not the exception but taken for granted

That the Irishman rides with a light bridle and lets it very much alone is the necessary result. His pace at the fences must be slow, because it is not a horse's nature, however rash, to rush at a place like the side of a house; and instinct prompts the animal to collect itself without restraint from a rider's hand, while any interference during the second and downward spring would only tend to pull it back into the chasm it is doing its best to clear.

The efforts by which an Irish hunter surmounts these national impediments is like that of a hound jumping a wall. The horse leaps to the top with fore-and-hind feet together, where it dwells, almost imperceptibly, while shifting the purchase, or 'changing', as the natives call it, in the shortest possible stride, of a few inches at most, to make the second spring. Every good English hunter will strike back with his hind legs when surprised into sudden exertion, but only a proficient bred, or at least, taught in the sister island, can master the feat described above in such artistic form . . .

But the merit is not heaven-born. On the contrary, it seems the result of patient and judicious tuition, called by Irish breakers 'training', in which they show much knowledge of character and sound common sense.

In some counties, such as Roscommon and Connemara, the brood mare indeed, with the foal at her foot, runs wild over extensive districts, and, finding no gates against which to lean, leaps leisurely from pasture to pasture, pausing, perhaps, in her transit to crop the sweeter herbage from some bank on which she is perched. Where mamma goes her little one dutifully follows, imitating the maternal motions, and as a charming mother almost always has a charming daughter, so, from its earliest foalhood, the future hunter acquires an activity, courage, and sagacity that shall hereafter become the admiration of crowded hunting-fields in the land of the Saxon far, far away!

But whereas in many parts of Ireland improved agriculture denies space for the unrestrained vagaries of these early lessons, a judicious system is adopted that substitutes artificial education for that of nature. 'It is wonderful we don't get more falls,' said one of the boldest and best of lady riders . . . 'when we consider that we all ride half-broken horses,' and, no doubt, on our side of the Channel, the observation contained a great deal of truth. But in this respect our neighbours show more wisdom. They seldom bring a pupil into the hunting-field till the elementary discipline has been gone through that teaches him when he comes to his fence *what to do with it*. He may be three, he may be four. I have seen a sportsman in Kilkenny so unassumingly equipped that instead of boots he wore wisps of straw called, I believe, '*sooghauns*',

go in front for a quarter of an hour on a two-year old! Whatever his age, the colt shows himself an experienced hunter when it is necessary to leap. Not yet *mouthed*, with unformed paces and wandering action, he may seem the merest baby on the road or across a field, but no veteran can be wiser or steadier when he comes within distance of it, or, as his owner would say, when he 'challenges' his leap, and this enthusiast hardly over-states the truth in affirming that his pupil 'would change on the edge of a razor, and never let ye know he was off the Queen's high-road, God bless her, all the time!'

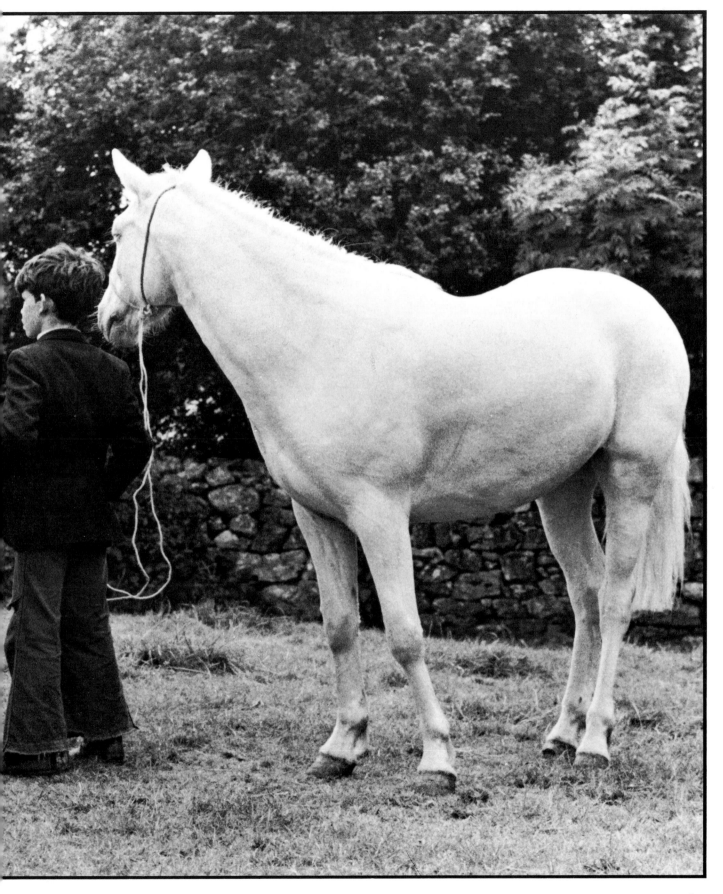

A mouth of iron

There are still moments when I can find some special and not-otherwise-to-be-attained flavour in driving on an outside car: a sense of personal achievement in sitting, by some method of instinctive suction, the lurches and swoops peculiar to these vehicles. Reardon's had given us its roomiest car and its best horse, a yellow mare, with a long back and a slinging trot, and a mouth of iron.

'Where did Mr Reardon get the mare, Jerry?' asked M'Cabe, as we zigzagged in successive hairbreadths through the streets of Owenford.

'D-Dublin, sir,' replied the driver, who, with both fists extended in front of him and both heels planted against his narrow footboard, seemed to find utterance difficult.

'She's a goer!' said M'Cabe.

'She is – she killed two men,' said Jerry, in two jerks.

'That's a great credit to her. What way did she do it?'

'P-pulled the lungs out o' them!' ejaculated Jerry, turning the last corner and giving the mare a shade more of her head, as a tribute, perhaps, to her prowess.

She swung us for some six miles along the ruts of the coast road at the same unflinching pace, after which, turning inland and uphill, we began the climb of four miles into the mountains. It was about eleven o'clock when we pulled up beside a long and reedy pool, high up in the heather; the road went on, illimitably it seemed, and was lost, with its attendant telegraph posts, in cloud.

'Away with ye now, Jerry,' said M'Cabe; 'we'll shoot our way home.'

He opened the back of the dog-box, and summoned its occupant. The summons was disregarded. Far back in the box two sparks of light and a dead silence indicated the presence of the dog.

'How snug you are in there!' said M'Cabe; 'here, Jerry, pull him out for us. What the deuce is this his name is? Jeffers told me yesterday, and it's gone from me.'

'I d'no would he bite me?' said Jerry, taking a cautious observation and giving voice to the feelings of the party. 'Here, poor fellow! Here, good lad!'

The good lad remained immovable. The lure of a sandwich produced no better result.

'We can't be losing our day with the brute this way,' said M'Cabe. 'Tip up the car. He'll come out then, and no thanks to him.'

As the shafts rose heavenwards, the law of gravitation proved too much for the setter, and he slowly slid to earth.

'If I only knew your dam' name we'd be all right now,' said M'Cabe.

The carman dropped the shafts on to the mare, and drove on up the pass, with one side of the car turned up and himself on the other. The yellow mare had, it seemed only begun her day's work. A prophetic instinct, of the reliable kind that is strictly founded on facts, warned me that we might live to regret her departure.*

* From Somerville and Ross, see Note, p. 187.

What is part of everyday life for the tinker is a great attraction for the tourist.
An exciting jaunt across Ireland in a horse-drawn caravan is now offered by nearly all
tour organizers

7

Famous Irish Horses

Sultan's skill

There now remained but one bank, the trampled remnant of the furze hurdle, and the stone wall. The pace was beginning to improve, and the other horses drew away from Sultan; they charged the bank at full gallop, the black mare and the chestnut flying it perilously, with a windmill flourish of legs and arms from their riders, the white horse racing up to it with a gallantry that deserted him at the critical moment, with the result that his rider turned a somersault over his head and landed, amidst the roars of the onlookers, sitting on the fence facing his horse's nose. With creditable presence of mind he remained on the bank, towed the horse over, scrambled on to his back again, and started afresh . . .

'There'll be a smash when they come to the wall! If one falls they'll all go!' panted Sally. 'Oh! – Now! Flurry! Flurry! –'

What had happened was that the chestnut colt had suddenly perceived that the gate at right angles to the wall was standing wide open, and, swinging away from the jump, he had bolted headlong out on to the road, and along it at top speed for his home. After him fled Canty's black mare, and with her, carried away by the spirit of stampede, went the white horse.

Flurry stood up in his stirrups and gave a view-halloa as he cantered down to the wall. Sultan came at it with the send of the hill behind him, and jumped it with a skill that intensified, if that were possible, the volume of laughter and yells around us. By the time the black mare and the white horse had returned and ignominiously bundled over the wall to finish as they might, Flurry was leading Sultan towards us.*

* From Somerville and Ross, see Note, p. 187.

170

In his book *The Kingdom of the Horse*, Hans-Heinrich Isenbart writes:

It is hard to imagine today that a rider once rode his horse over obstacles like a clothespin sits on a line. Yet, at the beginning of the present century, riders still soared across fences and ditches leaning backwards, holding on with clenched legs, and clinging to the reins of their tormented horses. The horse, repressed before the jump by violent jerking of the reins, catapulted himself across the obstacle, completely tense and greatly distressed.

The ability to use natural balance to develop power, and the adaptation of the rider to the jumping trajectory of the horse were introduced into equitation by Captain Frederico Caprilli, an Italian, who based his doctrine of the 'Natural Method' on observations of horses jumping in liberty.

In retrospect the happy coincidence that Frederico Caprilli used an Irish horse, La Piccola Lark, to demonstrate his Natural Method, can be seen as an indication of things to come, for this special relationship between an Italian rider and an Irish horse marked the beginning of teamwork which, in the past twenty years, has given us unforgettable moments in international show-jumping.

The question as to who was the greatest show-jumper of all times is impossible to answer. The name of the American, William Steinkraus, might come to mind, as would that of Hans Günther Winkler from Germany, or of the d'Inzeos, in particular Raimondo d'Inzeo, that incomparable artiste of the saddle who has carried on Caprilli's methods and expertise into the present.

These he has perfected on Irish horses, getting to know their characters, and making them feel at ease when ridden by him in the paddock. Complete harmony, freedom of gesture, precise informality, all were demonstrated effectively by Raimondo d'Inzeo on Gone Away and Bellevue in turn over the decades, and, somewhat in his shadow, by Graziano Mancinelli and Vittorio Orlandi who, with horses like Ambassador, Turvey and Fulmer Feather Duster increased the fame of Irish horses.

Previous page: L'Escargot (with the white noseband) with Tommy Carberry riding to victory in the Cheltenham Gold Cup of 1971. In 1975 they won the Aintree Grand National

The Olympic Games, Rome 1960: in the British team, Pat Smythe rode Flanagan, the horse which brought fame to its talented, and, in the finest sense of the word popular rider, a horse, whose birth, as we know, was the result of its dam 'kicking over the traces'. An 'Irish' unforeseen event with a successful outcome . . . Pat Smythe describes her ride in the Olympic Stadium in Rome:

It soon came round to Flanagan's turn, and I was feeling that it was a bit unkind to ask him to jump a course beyond his physical capabilities. He soon dispelled that fear, taking on the fences like a lion. Unfortunately he tried to take only one stride in the last part of the treble in spite of my firm restraint, obviously thinking, as did many other top horses, that the set distance was hardly credible without themselves or the fences falling, but lack of experience or intelligence seemed to be almost an asset with this trick distance. Flanagan had already landed almost at the foot of the third element of the treble and the big parallels. How he kept his feet while in that tangle of bars is more than I can imagine. I have a film of this round which tells its own story . . .

He jumped the next fence clear – a wide parallel bars over water. That afternoon he was less fresh and more obedient and so we negotiated the treble without fault. It had caused as much trouble to good horses as to the bad ones and a few riders did not enjoy the effect of their falls there. Flanagan, having as nearly come to grief in the morning, still retained his sense and courage to try his utmost in the afternoon. He almost stood on his head to get over the third part of the treble, and somehow he succeeded.

It proved his tremendous courage that he should tackle that fence without fear. Instead of being frightened by his bad mistake in the morning which must have hurt him, he had learned from it. Retaining all his boldness, he realized that he would have to obey me.

The successes of Irish horses on the racecourse are innumerable. Each has been brought about by careful training and is the result of an age-old breeding tradition.

However, chance plays a part too. This was particularly evident in 1932 in the stables of the Aga Khan. It was an English breeder, Lord Wavertree who first persuaded the eastern Nabob to dedicate himself to the turf, because, as he said, there were few other types of sport which could be compared with 'The Sport of Kings'. Lord Wavertree once wrote that Nature could only be controlled by human common-sense, and not by magic.

In 1921 the Aga Khan's first horse ran, but it took until 1925 before he won his first Derby.

In 1932, he bought a young foal in Ireland which was very nearly killed because of lung-trouble. This acquisition reached the racing stable very late. It was named Bahram after the Great Hunter in the Persian epic. Bahram was one of the few horses never to be beaten. It won in style all its nine races, including the famous 'Triple Crown' – the Derby, the 2000 guineas and the St Leger.

The Three-day Event is known as the 'Crown of Equitation'. In this most taxing area of equestrian sport, Irish horses have also time and again proved best. Here, perhaps, patience and care in training are more vital than in any other area.

Who can forget, for example, the overwhelming victory for the Italians at the Olympic Three-day Event at Karuizawa, Tokyo, in 1964? Not only did three young riders come to the fore – Marco Checcoli, Paolo Angioni and Giuseppe Ravano – but also three completely new horses, Irish horses – the nine-year-old white gelding Sunbeam, the eight-year-old King, and Royal Love, a ten-year-old. Together they were the big surprise of Karuizawa. They won the team gold medal from the USA and Germany, and Marco Checcoli and Sunbeam carried off the individual prize. These were days of triumph for the young riders, demonstrating the modern Italian method of show-jumping, and also days of triumph for Irish horses. Moreover, there was no question of their success being just an unexpected stroke of luck.

In 1956 in Stockholm and even more so in 1960 in Rome, the cross-country test was severely criticized for being barely within the limits of any horse's ability, and in some cases, for example, in Pratoni del Vivaro, beyond them.

As far as the Swiss were concerned, the Olympic Three-day Event in Rome was best of all. Silver in the team competition for Hans Schwarzenbach, Rudolf Günthard and Anton Bühler, and bronze in the individual award for Anton Bühler.

Anton Bühler was riding Gay Spark, an Irish horse.

Bühler has recorded his many years of experience in a book named, fittingly enough, *Doch zählen nicht allein die Siege* (It's not winning that really counts). Among his varied experiences, he describes in the form of a day-by-day diary, how he prepared Gay Spark for the Three-day Event. It is characteristic of a good rider to be able to describe in detail the preparation and training which he has carried out with a successful horse, in such a way that his readers not only understand the methods he used, but also come to know the nature of the horse.

Anton Bühler:

When I began the training of my Irish gelding, Gay Spark, for the all-important qualifying trials, I started to keep a diary, as I had done on previous occasions, in which I made note of anything that happened or of any observations I made at the time, thinking that it might be of some use at a later date.

The horse was then ten years old, and since 1956 had received an ideally graded training, having taken numerous easy and middle-range Three-day Event tests, and, in many ways, he had fulfilled the promise of talent he had shown. Strangely enough, though, he had never been entered for the more difficult trials.

In 1959, however, his whole training had been interrupted as a result of a lameness which was never properly localized. This break in his training schedule lasted until the February of the following year.

The first entry in my diary is for 17 February 1960: 'I'm glad to say that Gay Spark can take up his training again.'

By this time, I was convinced that Gay Spark would pass the difficult selection test which was to take place at the beginning of July in Aarau. I was also aware that what was most important in the coming months was that he remained in good health and spirits. I had often heard of cases where hopes had been dashed just before a competition because a horse had been over-taxed in the last few weeks of training, its drive worn out, or, worse still, because an injury had put it out of the running for ever.

I decided that the best training schedule for him should include numerous mountainside trotting sessions; long, quiet work on a special training programme for the cross-country test and a few gallops over middle distances.

The special training programme for the cross-country test was as follows:

I arranged to have a moveable and easily manipulated jump

Raimondo d'Inzeo (Italy) on Gone Away

Graham Fletcher (GB) on Buttevant Boy

Markus Fuchs (Switzerland) on Ballymena

Raimondo d'Inzeo (Italy) on Bellevue

Pat Taaffe on Arkle

Lester Piggott on My Swallow

Juliet Jobling Purser (Ireland) on Jenny

Graziano Mancinelli (Italy) on Ambassador

Harvey Smith (GB) on Mattie Brown

Chris Collins (GB) on Smokey

Piero d'Inzeo (Italy) on Easter Light

Michael Bullen (GB) on Wayfarer at the Burghley Trials in 1971

David Broome (GB) on Manhattan (now called Jaegermeister)

*At the international driver competition in Frauenfeld in 1974, J. Collinson (GB)
drove a four in hand with Vodka, Sam, Lime and Scott, all Irish geldings born in 1965*

brought out into the country. By combining this with the natural features of the land, I could build every combination of obstacle imaginable. For example, I placed it at the foot or on the upper ridge of a steep slope, half-way up an embankment, immediately following a downward slide or just before jumping up on a bank, in the middle of a wide, deep trench or behind a sharp bend and in other equally difficult positions.

In this way, my horse gradually learned to accept the unexpected, and soon, without any preparation whatsoever, he could approach and clear even the most daunting of fences with confidence.

This work was often carried out on bright summer mornings and was a constant source of enjoyment for me. We got to know each other better, we learned together and soon it looked as though we were ready to undertake anything.

I must point out again that at that time, mid-July, Gay Spark had not yet reached the top of his form. This was purposely planned, for if he had reached his peak then, how could it be kept up until September?

The preliminary selection trials took place in Aarau in mid-July. Gay Spark was at his best in the quadrangle; in this area, at least, he was accepted. However, in the very difficult cross-country test, I rode him very carefully, for, although our place on the team was at stake, I did not want to put him in any danger of injury.

At a rather treacherous combination of double posts and rails, we did a perfect head-over-heels, and, rein in hand, I landed in the grass. No harm! One can never be too sure of oneself in this kind of event; each jump is new and different and must be approached accordingly. The preliminary selection for Rome was made shortly after that: we'd made it!

Up to now, only the triumphs have been recorded in this chapter. They are seldom far from tragedy, however.

Every year, victims are claimed on thousands of the world's racecourses and show-jumping rings. Many unnamed horses fall on small rural courses. However, the amount of pain and sympathy afforded is not determined by the importance of the event; a tragedy is not lessened because it did not occur during an international meeting.

Nevertheless, a combination of the circumstances can multiply the shock: the scene is the International Riding and Show-Jumping Tournament of Aachen in July 1967. The final day, brilliant sunshine, a sell out, high expectations, the Aachen Grand Prix, coveted as few other prizes are, had reached its deciding phase.

Among the favourites were Graziano Mancinelli and his famous horse Turvey. The Irish horse was the darling of the public; he fascinated them with his downright, marked personality.

And then it happened.

Turvey was a star and knew it. With the relaxed composure of one used to success, he surveyed the course and the two or three fences nearest to him, while his rider saluted the judges. For a number of seconds, he kept this pose, like a monument, conscious of being the centre of attention, conceited, his head almost level, rein hanging loose between his mouth and his rider's hand.

I had seen Turvey like this hundreds of times before. Under Graziano Mancinelli he had become one of the world's best show-jumpers. There was hardly an important prize anywhere he had not won. He was to be the mainstay of the Italian equestrian team for the Mexico Olympics. All hopes were centred on him.

But in Soers in Aachen, the most splendid show-jumping grounds in Europe, near the point of winning the Grand Prix of Aachen, one of the few prizes not included among his conquests, he collapsed in front of 40,000 onlookers. The veterinary term for the cause: rupturing of the aorta.

Graziano Mancinelli, whom I had never once seen smile during the hundreds of competitions I had watched, whose face had never registered the bitterness felt at defeat and who had always seemed to be wearing a mask, wept unashamedly. He did not make the slightest effort to restrain himself, and 40,000 citizens of Aachen and millions viewing on television saw tears on the face of a man from whom they would have expected anything but helplessness when confronted with pain.

Turvey lay on the short side of the course. It was only a few minutes – but they seemed like hours – before the transporter came for him.

Once the dead horse had been removed from the stadium, his rider, helped by friends to the exit, began to recover from the shock.

The competition continued. Half an hour later a victor was acclaimed, albeit in a somewhat dampened fashion.

But then, the people of Aachen are among the fairest and most sympathetic sports public in the world.

Mr Softee was another Irish horse to win innumerable competitions. His success was, to a large extent, due to David Broome. Broome, utterly unsentimental in every way, could totally overcome nervousness. He came across the horse which was to partner him over the years by pure chance. It was owned by John Massarella.

Scene: The Royal International at the White City Stadium, London.

David Broome, in his book *Jump Off* (co-author Genevieve Murphy), wrote:

At the Royal International that year the horse had a fall on the opening day of the show and another, two days later, in the King's Cup. As a result of the second fall, John Lanni was carried out of the ring on a stretcher and taken straight to hospital. As everyone is taught, from their Pony Club days onwards, a horse tends to remember this sort of incident – especially if he is led straight back to his stable, without being given a reassuring 'pop' beforehand.

For this reason, and because John Lanni was out of action, Father said to John Massarella, 'If you want someone to give Softee a jump, just to get his confidence back, I'll go and get David.' I therefore had my first ride on Mister Softee in the collecting ring at White City, but it seemed an insignificant event at the time; I just cantered the horse round quietly, gave him a few 'pops' over some poles, and handed him back to the groom. Mr Massarella, who had been watching, didn't suggest that I should ride Softee again, so I thought nothing more about it.

This did not last long, however, because a few weeks later David Broome was to ride Mr Softee again. The years 1964 and 1965 were particularly successful for the two of them: among other prizes they won the four most important competitions in England – the King's Cup, the Show-Jumping Derby, the Olympic trials and first prize in the Horse of the Year Show.

A further episode in the professional career of these two stars is worth relating. It took place during the Mexico Olympics in 1968. The British team suffered a great set-back when Marion Coakes on her pony Stroller was eliminated in the second round of the Nations Cup, after two refusals and having exceeded the maximum time limit.

David Broome had not yet taken his second round. Here he describes those bitter moments:

In Mexico, where my second-round score was immaterial after Marion's elimination, I would have been happy to leave Mister Softee in his stable for the entire afternoon. My whole attitude was to get round as safely as possible – and out the other end; I had completely lost my enthusiasm. Even so, the Olympic atmosphere affected me . . .

Mister Softee was delighted with this enormous audience. He walked out into that pit, with a hundred thousand pairs of eyes looking down on him, and sized the whole thing up – the colour, the crowds, the buzz of excitement. As we waited in the centre of the ring, while a fence was rebuilt, he stood quietly, looking all around; it was almost as though he were sticking out his chest and saying, 'I'll show them who's champ.' . . .

Although I had jumped in a packed Olympic Stadium twice before, the atmosphere in Mexico still threw me slightly off balance as I began on my second round; I kept meeting fences on a shortening stride until I snapped to, and told myself, 'If we keep on like this, we're never going to make the combination.' Luckily there was a fence beforehand which I could have a bit of a cut at so I picked up my stick and chased Softee over it. This got him moving forward and he was absolutely right for the combination when it came, we only had the back part down.

We finished that round with twelve faults and, individually, Softee had the second best score of the day, with a total of twenty faults to Alwin Schockemöhle and Donald Rex's eighteen and three-quarters.

As we have already explained, many, many famous names are missing here, horses which have made Ireland's name throughout the world, just as much as those mentioned and photographed in this chapter.

It is part of the make-up of the Irish to be equally grateful to those horses which would never be mentioned in a sports book or in a book such as this, even though they have truly earned it. This implicit gratitude speaks louder than any printed eulogy; it is . . . Irish Horsemanship!

'Top-class performance in (equestrian) sport does not consist of the radical suppression of the spontaneity of an animal's drive by human influence, nor does it simply mean the total dominance of a human (over the horse). It is the result of a particularly happy combination of influence and adaptation.'

Heinz Meyer, *Mensch und Pferd*

Top-class performances are not the main topic of this book. Even though it cannot be denied that Irish horses have always achieved success in all areas of activity, these achievements are nevertheless peripheral to what we are trying to portray – the special, unique relationship which exists between the Irish and their horses.

Words such as 'special' and 'unique' will be read with mistrust by anyone who knows Ireland; not because they would doubt the qualities which warrant the Irish being thus described, but because they understand the Irishman's own mistrust of such words. Superlatives are always to be questioned when they express something which is self-evident.

For those who love Ireland and her horses, an encounter with Ireland and her horses is an invaluable experience.

For this is a case where love is *not* blind. On the contrary, it opens one's eyes to the easy-going affection between man and horse, and allows one to see it in the eyes of the Irish – as part of everyday life.

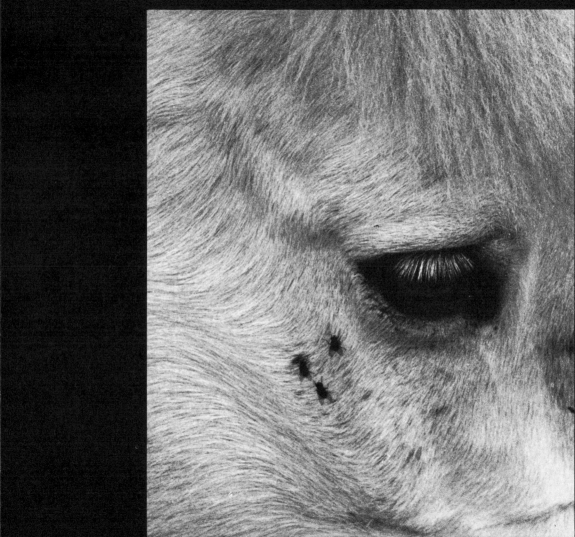

Acknowledgements

From the time we started the first preparations for this book to when we finally submitted the photographs and text, we have been a nuisance to a large number of people (and horses!). To these we should like to offer our thanks.

Dr Hans-Ulrich Staub, editor-in-chief of the 'Schweizer Kavallerist', helped us over the first hurdles, and also many subsequent ones. He made many invaluable contacts with people involved in Irish equestrian life and generously gave us access to a large amount of authentic material from the series *People and Horses*, published by the 'Schweizer Kavallerist' in Pfäffikon.

The contributions of both Bórd na gCapall (The Irish Horse Board) and Bórd Fáilte (The Irish Tourist Board) were vital to the success of the book. In particular Pat Dunne and Joe Lynam helped us time and again with our work as did Dermot Forde of Bórd na gCapall. They procured for us, among other items, the photographs of 'Famous Irish Horses' on p. 171 and pp. 174–7, the hunting scenes on pp. 90–93, and the picture of the Irish Draught. Permission to reproduce these photographs were kindly granted by the following photographers and agencies: Finlay Davidson, Coventry; Peter Sweetman, Naas; Leslie Lane, Burgess Hill, Sussex; Co-Press-Studio, Amsterdam, and Sport & General Agency, London.

We wish to extend our heartfelt thanks to the management of the National Stud in Tully, near Kildare. We spent our second night in Ireland in a stable box there, and were permitted to photograph the birth of a foal in the early hours of the morning.

In the Army training grounds in the Phoenix Park, we had the opportunity to observe horses going through their morning jumping routine.

We would also like to acknowledge the help of the following people: the directors of 'Ballykisteen' Stud in County Tipperary, 'Ardoons' in County Limerick and 'Mylerstown' in County Kildare; the directors of the race courses at Naas, the Curragh, the Phoenix Park, Mallow and Laytown, and also those responsible for the show-jumping competitions in Cork, Ballintreena, Galway, Blanchardstown, Waterford and Tipperary.

The Director of the Army Riding School, Lt-Col William Ringrose and trainer Erich Bubbel gave us much of their time, as did the Manager of the Irish National Stud, Michael Osborne.

For the section on thoroughbred sport and breeding, we owe our thanks to Bart J. Bastable and Maurice O'Brien of the Irish Hospitals' Sweepstakes; J. Irwin and P. Myerscough told us about Goff's Bloodstock Sales, and Lord Holmpatrick of the Turf Club and P. Walsh of the Racing Board gave us insight into the technical and administrative aspects of racing.

We thank John Daly for the opportunity to take the most beautiful pictures and for his wonderful friendship.

We also spent unforgettable days with the Master of the Hounds, Thady Ryan and his wife, an excellent cook, at Scarteen, near Tipperary.

Thanks are also due to Marco Tissi for his photographs of landscape and houses on pp. 16–17, 103, 136 and 137.

We would like to thank Ruedi Homberger, the then Director of the Kundig Travel Agency in Zurich, Hans Hunziker, and the Aer Lingus representative in Switzerland, Lou Hehrensperger, for finding valuable contacts for us in Ireland. We are also grateful to them for their continuing help with our travel arrangements.

Finally, we extend our thanks to Hans Bodenmüller in Aesch for his readiness to share with us his years of experience with Irish horses, and to Karl Erb in Forch for allowing us access to his sporting records.

Last of all, we wish, of course, to acknowledge our debt to the innumerable O'Briens, O'Malleys, O'Connors and Kellys who were always ready to offer us advice, be it in the stables, among the crowds at the races or out in the paddocks and who taught us, in pubs, amidst beer glasses and singing, to love this land, these people and these horses.

Monique and Hans D. Dossenbach
Hanspeter Meier
Max Rüeger

Note

The publishers thank the following for permission to reproduce copyright material: John Farquharson Ltd for extracts from *The Complete Experiences of an Irish RM* by Somerville and Ross on pp. 12, 28, 48, 72, 86, 98, 130, 166, 170 and also for extracts from *Flanagan, My Friend* by Pat Smythe on pp. 146, 149, 172; Collins Publishers for the extract from *The Kingdom of the Horse* by H. H. Isenbart and E. M. Bührer on pp. 172, 173, 179; A. M. Heath and Hutchinson Publishing Group for the extracts from *Jump Off* by David Broome and Genevieve Murphy on p. 180; and the Poolbeg Press for the extract from Michael McLaverty's story *The White Mare* on pp. 134–5, 142.

Slán Leat

Information

Racecourses
The annual racing programme, with approximately 180 races on thirty-one courses, is available from the Irish Tourist Board. See address below.

Riding Schools
There are about seventy riding schools in Ireland, some of which also arrange treks lasting several days. A useful booklet *Where to Ride in Ireland*, is published by Bórd na gCapall, The Irish Horse Board. See address below.

Horse-drawn Caravan Centres
Covered wagons and draught horses can be hired in these centres. They can be returned at the end of the holidays at whichever depot is nearest.

Fox-Hunting
The fox-hunting season is from the beginning of November to the end of March. There are also Cubbing Meets on which young horses and young hounds are trained. The cub-hunting season lasts from 1 September to 31 October.

Hare-Hunting
The hare-hunting season also lasts from the beginning of November to the end of March. 'Beagling' – hare-hunting on foot – is also common.

Further information on the various equestrian sport events, riding or horse drawn caravan holidays is available from:
> Irish Tourist Board
> Baggot Street Bridge
> Dublin 2
> IRELAND

Information on horse auctions, horses and ponies for sale and how to buy them is available from:
> Irish Horse Board
> St Mealruan's
> Tallaght
> County Dublin
> IRELAND